Living Love

May happiness always
find you!
Maetreyii Ma

Living Love

The Yoga of Yama & Niyama

Timeless Teachings
for Transformation and Awakening

Maetreyii Ma

Published by
Ananda Guru Kula Publications
P.O. Box 9655, Santa Rosa, California 95405

Editing and Compilation:
Maetreyii Ma, Virginia May, Sita (Sylvia Hawley)

Cover Art & Design:
Kalleheikki Kannisto, Rectoverso Graphic Design

Dedicated to
My Beloved Baba

About Baba

How These Writings Came to Be

I first began to be aware of a divine presence as a young girl, perhaps around eleven or twelve. I didn't know anything about past lives but when I felt this presence, I was sure I had known him before. It was distinctly male, clearly divine and seemed to be dressed in white, emanating waves of compassion and unconditional love. I immediately fell in love. He was my guide, my comfort in the storms of life. He healed me when I was hurt, walked with me when I was alone. He was so kind. How could anyone not love him?

The years passed and I became involved with the normal social life of an American teen and forgot about these experiences until in my early twenties I learned meditation in an eastern yogic tradition. After some months of doing regular meditation, I began to have experiences of non-ordinary states of consciousness and again this numinous divine presence came to me.

This time he talked to me and revealed more of his nature. In his every word I experienced the emanations of perfect justice, divine love and absolute beauty. Like the rays of the sun shining through a prism, his divine aspects revealed themselves. His nature, revealed before me, was shining with brilliant light that stunned my mind. The experience of waves of divine love washed through my being. For many years he taught me, sheltered me in the storms of life, held me in my darkest hours and revealed to me the bliss of divine love in which all is one unitary whole.

When I first met him as a child, I thought he was Jesus and I cried that I had missed him and was here without him. Then later when he came in my twenties, he called himself Baba. I thought he was the inner expression of my Guru, Shrii Shrii Anandamurti. Sometimes I saw him as Krishna and sometimes as Shiva. In yoga, they say Guru, God and Self are one. He is for me most certainly that God Self, my beloved Guru Deva, my Baba.

I only saw my physical guru, Shrii Shrii Anandamurti Baba, for less than a year in the early 1970s. When I met him I felt the same blissful waves, the same presence I felt from my beloved Baba within. In *darshan*, guru's talks, often Anandamurti Baba would refer to things my Baba had told me and would explain them. They became one in the same, inner Guru and outer Guru. I knew then that truly Guru, God and Self are one.

The years passed and when, in 1990, my physical Guru, Shrii Shrii Anandamurti left his body, my inner Baba asked me to begin to share with others the teachings he had been giving to me for so long. I learned to sink into his flow of love and allow his words to come through me, not in channeling, but in an expression of divine grace some people call *Bhava*, a state of absorption in the Divine. This became the *Baba Talks* I have given ever since.

The writings in this book are directly inspired by the flow

of unconditional love and wisdom from my Baba. They are a fusion of my writing, his grace and the oral *Baba Talks* edited for readability. Divine grace and love inspire most of the writings contained in this book. I hope that you enjoy reading them as much as I have enjoyed the blissful experience of writing and editing them and that they help you along your path as they have helped me along mine.

Many Blessings,
Maetreyii Ma

Shrii Shrii Anandamurti Baba

Not everyone is fortunate enough to meet his or her guru in physical form. I feel blessed to have had this opportunity. My guru, Shrii Shrii Anandamurti walked this earth from 1921 until 1990. He lived in northern India, Bihar and Bengal, and taught in the ancient traditions of classical north Indian *Tantra* and *Asthanga Yoga*.

I had an opportunity to spend almost a year in India receiving his *darshan*, seeing him and hearing his talks, and had many profound experiences being near to him. Baba was reported to speak in two-hundred languages and could talk to all those who came to see him in their native tongues. I observed many miracles occurring around him – reports of him visiting people in one location while at the same time he was giving a talk at another nearly five-hundred miles away, people going into states of divine bliss simply from his glance, healings, people finding their hearts opened and their lives changed. Waves of divine bliss accompanied him when he entered a room and he knew everything about you, including your deepest core feelings. He was an ocean of love, a true realized Master. When people looked into his eyes, they saw the universe.

It was said that as a small boy of about five years while walking alone in the jungle, he encountered a pillar of white light. When he asked who it was, the pillar told him it was Shrii Shrii Anandamurti. When it enfolded him in the light, the boy became the Master.

Preface

The nature of the oral text in this book has been preserved in its editing. Additional material has been added to enhance the readability and to add clarity and relevant content. A few Sanskrit terms important to yogic philosophy and practice are used, as their meaning is more precise in Sanskrit. They are usually defined immediately after the word. However, for the convenience of readers wanting more extensive definitions or who are not familiar with these terms, they are also defined in a glossary at the end of the book.

Table of Contents

Introduction

*A*s a clinical psychologist and teacher in the yogic tradition, I have great appreciation for the depth of psychological wisdom yoga has to offer. My studies in transpersonal psychology and my clinical practice have intertwined with years of meditation and study of yogic wisdom to bring me to the understanding of the teachings put forward in this work. However, the deepest influence is the divine presence and flow of intuitive knowledge from my wisdom Source, my beloved Guru Deva.

Yoga is an ancient system of teachings and practices for transformation and awakening. The teachings date back over five-thousand years and were developed to support transformation from an ego-centered awareness to knowledge and direct personal experience of the numinous. The meaning of the term yoga is literally "to yoke," that is to unite our small sense of self with divine omnipresent Consciousness.

Patanjali, often called the father of yoga, is credited with having codified three-thousand years of pre-existing yogic philosophy and practice into a seminal text called *The Yoga Sutras*, written in approximately 200 CE. In this text he expounds upon a system of spiritual practices known as *Ashtanga Yoga*, literally meaning the eight-limb path, referring to eight core areas of spiritual practice. *Asthanga Yoga* includes the practices of *Yama* and *Niyama* for learning how to embody spiritual values in our daily lives, *Asanas*, or yoga postures, for care of our bodies, *Pranayama* for harmonizing breath, body and mind, *Pratyahara,* for withdrawing attention from the thoughts and senses, *Dharana* for learning how to concentrate, *Dhyana,* meditation for directing the mind toward the divine Self and *Samadhi,* complete absorption in the eternal One.

The first two limbs of *Ashtanga Yoga, Yama* and *Niyama,* form a foundation of attitudes and behaviors that enable us to experience the enlightened awareness cultivated in meditative practices. *Yama* and *Niyama* address our psychology and how we act in the world. They are guidelines for self-development that focus our thoughts and our actions

THE EXPERIENCE OF ENLIGHTENED AWARENESS IS CULTIVATED IN MEDITATIVE PRACTICES.

so that we cultivate harmony and respect for all life, thus becoming able to grasp the deeper levels of our own being. They give clear guidelines on how to be in the world in a way that allows us to express our highest human potential.

Yama consists of five types of action to avoid, and their opposite attitude to cultivate, in our relationship to the world around us. They are: *Ahimsa* nonviolence, *Satya* truthfulness, *Asteya* non-stealing, *Brahmacharya* non-excess, and *Aparigraha* non-possessiveness. *Niyama* consists of five kinds of attitudes and actions we need to incorporate in our lives to be able to realize the Divine. They are: *Saucha* purity, *Santosha* contentment, *Tapas* selfless love, *Svadhyaya* knowledge of our real Self and *Ishvara Pranidhana* surrender to God.

These ten practices for living in the world form a cornerstone for a healthy, expansive psychology that enables a person to succeed in meditative practice. In Patanjali's yogic system, the practices of *Yama* and *Niyama* support our journey toward spiritual enlightenment by changing our relationship to ourselves and to the world around us. Yama and *Niyama* are living principles that are to be practiced, contemplated, witnessed and experienced. They are practical guidelines for self-development. These practices result in growing love, compassion, contentment, wisdom and ability to know the Divine.

There is an underlying unity in the practices of *Yama* and *Niyama*. As they are practiced over time, they create a complex system of personal and social integrity that is particularly adaptable to and needed in contemporary culture. By appreciating the links between all of these practices, spiritual aspirants can experience an integrated development of life as a whole. When practiced sincerely and regularly, *Yama* and *Niyama* promote deep understanding and care for the welfare of living beings as well as spiritual connection.

This book, based on Patanjali's original tenets, is written in a style that is meant to be easily understood. It offers a guide for daily life and the journey toward Divine connection. The first chapter of the book begins with an exploration of spiritual life and how *Yama* and *Niyama* provide a foundation. Chapters Two and Three present extensive discussion and insights about the application of the five avoidances of *Yama* and the five observances of the *Niyama*. Chapter Four explores the application of spiritual practice in our lives, increasing our capacity to love, forgive, feel compassion and express gratitude. Chapter Five gives insight into the dynamics of power and survival instincts in our families, group affiliations and societies. It explores the validity of ethical codes in the face of human instincts. The next two chapters give insight into how to work with our psychological issues and practice *dharma* (the way), service, love and happiness. The final chapter gives down to earth exercises for applying these practices for self-development.

The teachings in the book can be of value to anyone seeking spiritual wisdom and self-development. While based in the practices of *Ashtanga Yoga*, the truths held within these pages are universal, and not limited to those who are engaged in yoga. The practices of *Yama* and *Niyama* are for anyone that wants to lead a more loving, honest, self-confident and conflict-free life.

CHAPTER I

Living Love

"Oh my heart! The Supreme Spirit,
The great Master is near you: wake, oh wake!
Run to the feet of your Beloved,
For your Lord stands near to your head.
You have slept for unnumbered ages;
This morning will you not wake?"
SONGS OF KABIR BY TAGORE

*W*ithin the span of each and every person's life, a wide variety of experiences arise, some pleasant, some unpleasant, some neutral. Yet in every person's life there are moments when there is a direct connection to the Soul, to one's essence.

There are moments when you feel you have gone past your day-to-day engagements, your struggles and your difficulties, your joys, your relationships. You have gone deep within for a moment and touched something profound. Perhaps you feel expansiveness, a connection with nature, with all beings, perhaps with the stars in the heavens, perhaps with a loved one. For a moment, you transcend your ordinary way of looking at the world, the ordinary boundaries by which you define your-self and confine yourself and you become for a moment, free, unbound, alive, connected to your Soul, to your essence.

Your heart goes out in connection to all the living beings in the world, all the people, all the plants, all the animals and even the sunset, the mountains, the ocean. Have you ever felt yourself soar on the wings of an eagle, dive into the sea, rise with the sun, expand with the vastness of the universe? Have you ever contemplated all the planets and the multitude of living beings in the stars above? When you do you begin to realize how small is a human life, how fleeting and yet how precious each and every moment, because each and every moment is an opportunity to know the Infinite, to connect to the source of being. Each and every moment is an opportunity to expand your consciousness beyond the limits of your five senses and your physical body, to expand and become something more, something great, something amazing.

EACH AND EVERY MOMENT IS AN OPPORTUNITY TO KNOW YOUR INNERMOST SELF.

Each and every moment is an opportunity to know your innermost Self and through knowing that divine Self, you come to know the vastness of this whole creation. For all truly lies within, in the depths of your Soul. In the deep inner recesses of your being lies the unstruck music from which stars are born, planets come to exist and endless living beings move, are being born, live for a time and fade from this world. Countless beings are coming and going, all abiding in the chords of eternity and known in the depths of your own being.

There, the difference between I and thou dissolves. There, where light and sound are one, your experience is flooded with a shower of light. There, love abides, undefined,

22

unconfined. There love is an unconditional light, truth, being and the chord is a sound from which all creation unfolds. There, past, present and future meld together as one. There, all knowledge abides and the heart is fulfilled. There, lover and beloved become one and the weary traveler finds his or her home at last. In the sunrise, in the sunset, in the sound of the *THE SAGES OF THE PAST* robin flitting from limb to limb, *HAVE GIVEN US A MAP,* in the mountain, in the sea, in the *HAVE CHARTED THE DEEP* moment between then and now *WATERS AND FOUND A WAY* is the doorway to this uncharted *TO ACCESS THE VAST LOVE* land, the land of your Soul. So *WITHIN EACH OF US.* take heart, find your boat and sail the uncharted waters in the depths of your being to find the untouched shore of eternity and the unfettered essence of your own Self.

Meditation is a practice that allows you to quiet the restless mind so that you may listen within and traverse to the shores of the inner sea. The truth of meditation is always with you because it is your soul of souls; it is your very own Self; it is the love that has no beginning and no end, of which all relations of this world are but mirror reflections rising again and again always to remind you of the nature of your Soul. Take the time to journey within to those pristine halls where the unstruck music plays eternally. And remember for success, as in all journeys a way needs charting.

The sages of the past have given us a map, have charted the deep waters and found a way to access the vast love within each of us. In the ancient practices of *Yama* and *Niyama,* they have illumined a way to live in love in this very world. Understanding of the journey to living love in every moment of your life unfolds through these practices as you learn how to live with harmony and reverence for all life. With these practices you learn how to live without doing harm to others, to stand in truth, to see the Infinite all around and to be in peace and contentment. You discover how to love selflessly and surrender on the infinite shores of your soul's abode. These yogic practices work with the body and the mind to foster a ground for transformation of consciousness.

Dwelling in Infinite Love

Yama and Niyama practices are for the purpose of purifying the worldly vessel so that which is infinite, pure and untarnished may be perceived. They are like the cloth that is used to shine the mirror, taking off the dust and dirt so that the clear reflection of reality may be perceived.

Then, when the god of death (from the *Rig Veda*) *Yama*, comes to pay his call upon you, you may say to him, "Lord *Yama*, you are very powerful indeed but I have not wasted this life. I have purified my mind and body so that the perception of the Infinite has come to me. You will have to seek another, for though this body may pass from existence, I am beyond your reach. I dwell with the Divine in infinite love. You will have to go elsewhere, for I am not bound by the comings and goings of this finite world." The Lord *Yama* may not take what is not his, what has already been freed from the bondages of this world.

So if you want to know the Infinite and to go beyond the reach of death, follow the codes of spiritual life laid down long ago by those who have understood the workings of the mind and who have walked the journey before you. Follow these practices and rest your mind upon the Infinite. Then the peace and love inherent in all existence will be yours eternally.

Never think it is too difficult. It is your birthright, oh human being, to know Divinity. Walk forward without fear. Surely the grace of the Infinite will fall upon you and the strength you require will be given to you. So go forward with all your heart, following the codes of *Yama* and *Niyama*, keeping your mind ever fixed upon the Supreme, and that which you love will surely become your own.

CHAPTER II

Avoiding the Pitfalls

Yama

The tenets of Yama and Niyama are the essence of spiritual life. Within these tenets are held the core practices for those people who would aspire to know Brahma, the primal source of all being. These practices are intended to make the mind more supple so that it may be receptive to the subtle waves of the Infinite.

The practices of *Yama* explore those actions to be avoided in order to lead a noble life and be able to experience a connection to the Divine. They delve into the pitfalls of the human mind and direct us to the actions that will open the heart and bring us in harmony with all life. Thus they bring us to a deeper level of connectedness and wholeness that enables us to experience divine love and presence.

Ahimsa
Non-Injury

*"You might quiet the whole world
For a second if you pray.
And if you love, really love,
Our guns will wilt."*
St. John of the Cross

Ahimsa is the principle of non-injury or non-violence. It literally means not to do harm. Doing harm is the first and most basic of the five actions to avoid. The spirit of *Ahimsa* is one in which a person will not intentionally inflict pain or suffering upon another.

The practices of *Ahimsa* and of loving-kindness are inseparable. When you develop in *Ahimsa*, you naturally develop loving-kindness and compassion for all living beings. When you make a serious effort not to inflict harm by thought, word or deed what is left but acts of kindness? Loving-kindness and compassion are expressions of *Ahimsa* or non-injury because the opposite of injury is to treat with kindness and love all living beings. From this tenet of non-injury comes the idea of loving-kindness and compassion.

THE PRACTICES OF *AHIMSA* AND OF LOVING KINDNESS ARE INSEPARABLE.

Compassion
To do no harm and practice compassion is complex. To be compassionate does not mean simply to love everyone you

approve of, everyone except the bad people, except Hitler, or anyone else you are adverse to. Why is it so difficult to truly love everyone? Isn't it because you cannot accept them and isn't this because you cannot accept yourself? It is difficult to accept the shadow darkness, which is also part of life.

To have compassion does not mean that you only love the light and the qualities you like in yourself and others. Compassion does not reject or deny. It is an unconditional caring, a mode of being that affirms the deep spiritual essence of all beings and sees the suffering that causes people to inflict pain on others or on themselves. It also involves loving and accepting yourself as the beloved child of a loving God. To practice non-injury, to have compassion, empathy and understanding for the needs of all beings is essential to spiritual life and a natural result of spiritual life.

Yet there are times when you may need to make difficult choices, choices that may cause harm to one being to avoid harm to another. Be conscious of those choices. Make them with compassion for those beings that may be harmed by your action. As much as you can in all ways that you can, bring kindness to all beings.

Sometimes, someone, be they human or animal may annoy you. It is natural. You may even get angry under certain circumstances.

LET COMPASSION AND LOVING KINDNESS BE YOUR RUDDER IN THE STORM OF LIFE.

However, when you go inside yourself and consider what the world looks like from the eyes of the other, you gain compassion for their struggle. Then anger tends to dissipate and loving kindness returns. No one is an island. Everyone is a part of divine Consciousness. Everyone is a part of you and you are a part of them.

For example, when another does harm to you, you can take that harm into yourself and feel defensive and then angry, wanting to do harm back. However if you hold the situation with compassion, you will see that the one doing harm is acting out of his or her own ignorance and suffering. The harm they do binds them in that suffering. The harm done to others, they do to themselves.

When another does harm to you, understand with compassion the pain that is causing that person to do the ill deed. Send love that he or she may heal from the ignorance that has caused this wrong action. You do not have to accept the insults or harm directed toward you. You may not be able to change the bad circumstance or ill will, but you need not accept it, meaning let it go. Don't take it on.

Compassion does not mean to accept mistreatment but it does mean to respond with kindness. There are times when you may be tempted to do harm to another in retaliation. When this happens, realize that in this action you do harm to yourself. Not only theoretically, but actually, because the defensiveness of your being grows in magnitude. In trying to defend your ill actions and the pain you have caused others you can go very far afield in self-justification. Instead, let compassion and loving kindness be your rudder in the storm of life.

Intentions

All of the practices of *Yama* and *Niyama* take into account the intention behind the action. It is not the specific act that defines *Ahimsa,* but the intention that is followed. When your thoughts are kind and your intentions are for the welfare of all, *Ahimsa* naturally follows. When you have angry, revengeful thoughts or harmful intentions, be they of physical harm and brute force or psychological harm, *Ahimsa* will evade you. When you harm another intentionally to get what you want *Ahimsa* is lost.

To truly practice *Ahimsa*, you must practice from the intent. Two people may do the same action. For one it is harmful and against *Ahimsa*, and for another there is no injury done. The results depend upon the intentions of the person performing the action. For example, two people may run for a political office, each with the potential of filling that office. One person may be motivated by a strong sense of dedication to the welfare of the people served. Perhaps he wants to be in office so certain changes can be made for everyone's well-being. This person's intention is service to others. Another person running for the same office may be motivated by greed and a desire for self-importance and power rather than service or a good cause. Maybe he owns a company that will benefit greatly if he can get certain legislation passed.

Both individuals are engaged in the same actions but for very different reasons. The outcome of one or the other succeeding to office will be very different, as their motives differ. One will serve the welfare of the people to the best of his or her ability, while the other will do what is necessary to promote his own glory and as a result may do harm to those he has been elected to serve. Therefore, whether or not you actually injure others is not simply determined by what you do but also by why you do it.

In the practice of *Ahimsa* there is no intent to inflict pain or injury on another living being, passively or actively. Even, as in the above example, where there

INTENTIONS LEAD TO THOUGHTS THAT IGNITE PASSIONS THAT LEAD TO ACTIONS.

is not the intent of harm but intentions that compromise the needs of others for one's own benefit, injury can be the result. If there is intent to inflict injury, pain or suffering, then *Ahimsa* is lost altogether. If a person has injured you and you strike that person in return, with the intention to do injury, this is a violation of *Ahimsa*. Revenge is not the mode of a spiritual aspirant.

Intentions lead to thoughts that ignite passions that lead to actions. The mind is a monkey mind, a confusing complex of feelings, needs, thoughts and self-justifications. To know good from evil or right from wrong is often very confusing. Many times our beliefs and self-justifications can get in our way.

Judgment is a difficult bedfellow for one wanting to know the Divine. It tends to squash the tender strands of love that blossom from the heart. When we are busy judging others, we are usually not engaged in loving them. Often loving kindness goes out the window to be replaced by righteous anger or self-justifying thoughts of punishing the other. We then find ourselves engaged in intentions of harm toward another. *Ahimsa* escapes us when we put ourselves above another and stand in judgment of that person.

Yet there are times when we see things we truly believe are harmful to others or just plain wrong action being done by someone or by some group of people. How can one avoid judgment and practice compassion in the face of such situations? It takes subtlety of perception and a very kind heart as well as great strength of character not to engage in self-justifying judgments but instead, think with a calm and even mind what is for the greatest good of all involved and then act accordingly.

The deeper one's love for all living beings, the more established you are in *Ahimsa,* the more wisdom and objectivity will be reflected in your perceptions and conclusions. Let compassion be your meter to evaluate the situation. Let love and kindness be your rudder to show you the way to truth and right actions that do the least harm to everyone involved.

Working with Anger

There are times for all of us when we become angry. Anger is a basic defensive human emotion and part of the fight or flight response. When it is denied, it simply goes underground and can become passive-aggressive behavior or even backstabbing aggression done with a sweet smile. This is not compassion or loving kindness.

When anger arises it is best to acknowledge it, feel it, explore it, but if possible do not let it get the better of you. In most cases, it is best to be the witness of this strong emotion, breathe, take some space and do what you can to calm down while honoring your feelings before confronting the situation or person that has triggered you. When you are calm and can think clearly again, that is usually the best time to take action, as you will be more likely able to incorporate kindness and avoid doing harm.

Anger is not always bad or even hurtful. It is merely energy, energy that is sometimes needed to handle a situation. Denial or self-deprecation because of any emotion, including anger, can lead to self-harm and be destructive to one's self-esteem. Anger like all emotions can be used to harm or to help. Stand apart and observe your own motives and try to discern what is for the welfare of all involved and act accordingly. Utilize the energy of the anger for the good. But to do this, many times a little space is needed to be able to think clearly and be sure it is used for the highest good, not to inflict harm.

ANGER LIKE ALL EMOTIONS CAN BE USED TO HARM OR TO HELP.

When dealing with long-term situations in which you feel wrong is done to you or others and you feel helpless, anger may arise again and again. You may feel like a victim and the pain, hurt and helplessness make you want to hurt the aggressor who has harmed you. A gamut of emotions may arise over time from anger to grief, to fear, to deep hurt and if the anger turns inward, even depression may ensue. If these really difficult situations arise in your life, it is important to practice loving kindness and compassion toward yourself as you find your way out of darkness to your own personal strength and happiness. The challenge is to do no harm to yourself or to others in your helplessness and rage and instead to transmute the energy into a connection to your Higher Self and your own inner resilience, thus moving from fear and anger to hope and love.

Harm and Force

Non-injury and avoiding the use of force are not always the same. To defend your home against robbers is not necessarily a violation of *Ahimsa*, though you may need to use force against the aggressor. The person entering the house may come with harm in mind and, in defense of your family and home, you may need to use force to stop the intruder. Even though you may harm the individual, *Ahimsa* is not violated when the harm you do prevents a greater harm that may have occurred to loved ones in the home.

On the other hand, when physical harm is intentionally done to a person who has done nothing to you and is threatening no one, this is a strong violation of *Ahimsa*. If, because you do not like someone's philosophy, ideas or the way he or she talks to you, you attack either verbally or physically, you do harm. Harm is done when you become the aggressor, when you act in anger with mental or physical violence. Non-violence requires the rudder of loving kindness. When you lose it, take a moment to reflect on the deep divine nature of all beings and look with eyes of compassion at the imperfections of others.

Let the mind remain kind and compassionate. If it is the divine Self of all who has come in the form of another being, should you have mean and angry thoughts against them? No. Remember always that it is the one infinite Self that is manifesting in both the bright lights of this world and the shadows. Each and every person holds a spark of that divine essence. Everyone, no matter how misguided and destructive in taking actions, deep within is a child of the Great. So do not intend hurt or harm to anyone. If you must defend yourself or your family or even your community, you must do what you must do for the welfare of all.

To follow *Ahimsa*, lead a life in which you maintain a

kind and caring attitude toward all living beings. Why hurt a living being if you can avoid the injury? If you must hurt that being, then do it only under circumstances where it is unavoidable. And maintain a kind feeling for that being. You may be forced to act in an instance of self-defense or to defend your nation and your people against a violent assault. All of these things are not against *Ahimsa* when they represent the path of least harm. To stop a tyrant who is brutally harming many is not against *Ahimsa*, though it may require violence and force.

Violence and force are part and parcel of the cycle of life. When one creature dies, another is born. When life is coming into the world there is force in the process. There is violence and pain in birth. In the death of a living being oftentimes there is also force. One moves through life through the propulsion of the life force. There is no harm in this. Yet if that propulsion becomes mean-minded, is meant to harm or injure another and the qualities of hatred and dislike dominate the mind or the actions, then the tenets of *Yama* and *Niyama* are violated.

The Practice of Harmlessness

In this world you need to take practical measures to secure your existence. Food must be taken and your body washed. Everything you eat, even if it is only vegetables require the consumption of life. When you bathe, you inadvertently kill untold numbers of microbes. Each time your foot is placed upon the ground, so many microscopic entities may be harmed, yet the foot must be placed upon the ground if you are to walk. So relatively speaking, even though you may take an attitude of reverence and respect for all life, still a practical approach needs to be applied to live in this world.

Yet this practical approach needs to have some limitations. Randomly to take a life, be it a human life, a dog, a cat, or a little mouse, is an act of harm. Even the little ant should not be killed unless necessity and the welfare of human beings demand it. If it is merely for convenience, it is harm to living beings. If the ants are eating your food, if the mice bring disease, then the welfare of the people must be protected.

However, if at all possible, the welfare of the little creatures must also be protected. Do what you can to assist them in moving their residence. If still they will not, then measures might need to be taken to move them but only as a last resort should you harm them. For you must remember the little mouse loves its life, has its own children to feed and its own family to protect. Do not harm it unless there is no other choice. It too is a child of the Divine.

> *ALL THE CREATURES OF THIS WORLD ARE CHILDREN OF THE DIVINE.*

Likewise all the creatures of this world are children of the Divine. They all love their lives and want to survive and find happiness just as you do. The more developed and intelligent the living being is, the more he or she is capable of experiencing suffering and being hurt by cruel actions. So honoring the lives of not only human beings but of all beings, large and small, is part and parcel of *Ahimsa*.

To follow Ahimsa in dietary choices and inflict the least amount of pain on living beings, it is best to eat from the bottom of the food chain avoiding harm to animals. Eating nutritionally and caring for your own body is also a part of non-violence. Finding ways to do this with the least harm to other living beings makes your habits truly a practice of *Ahimsa*. Nonviolence in dietary choices sets you on a path to good health and the least harm to living beings.

If an attitude of not inflicting injury on living beings is maintained for a long period of time and reflected in your actions, then you will find that you have developed a compassionate heart. Love and sweetness will fill the mind. This compassion is a great gift from the Divine. When you are kind to living beings, when in your heart you have no malice or ill intent for anyone or anything, then you begin to understand the nature of love. Then you become capable of loving others. This is a part and parcel of *Ahimsa*.

Ahimsa in Social Movements

The yogic concept of *Ahimsa* has provided a base for some significant social movements in recent history. The practice of *Ahimsa* has become well known throughout the East and the West. It was a cornerstone of Gandhi's work to free India from British rule and was later picked up by Martin Luther King in his civil rights efforts of the 1960s in the United States. It was used in South Africa and continues to have a strong influence in movements for non-violent communication and non-violent conflict resolution.

IMAGINE A WORLD WHERE PEOPLE RESOLVE THEIR CONFLICTS WITH LOVING KINDNESS AND COMPASSION.

Its potential for interpersonal and even international application is profound. Imagine a world where people resolve their conflicts with loving kindness and compassion, really listening to each other, where the intent to do no harm and to support the welfare of all beings rules not only our individual but our collective actions. Imagine a world where reverence for all life is actually practiced and we live in harmony with all living beings.

The practice of *Ahimsa* is the key and it begins with each and every one of us, in every moment of every day. It begins when we start to place more value on love and kindness than we do on being right and winning. It begins when we take the time to notice the divine Self all around us, in everyone we meet, in all the living beings of this world and we open our hearts to love.

Satya
Benevolent Truthfulness

Satya is the practice of truthfulness and the second tenet of *Yama*. This is the practice of not deceiving oneself or others. Being truthful with others and with oneself is of utmost importance on the spiritual journey, as the goal of yoga is to know the ultimate truth.

Satya is not simply literal truth. It is compassionate truthfulness, the truth given with a sense of benevolence. This benevolent truthfulness imbues truth with the quality of *Ahimsa* or the intent of not doing harm. This is truth used to heal and to bring people toward their own deep love within, not to hurt or scar them.

On Lying

The opposite of *Satya* is deception, lying. Lying is a practice that can start out with small untruths to make life smoother with others, to avoid reactions to what you do, get things you want and so on. Maybe you started out learning to lie because you were shy or ashamed of yourself or didn't feel you could meet up to someone's expectations. Maybe you were afraid of getting in trouble and found that lying was the easy way out. Maybe you started hanging out with other people who lied to you and you learned to get ahead by following their example or yielding to the group norm. Maybe you simply wanted to be accepted and to look good to others finding that when you said what they wanted it just worked better. Or maybe you are the person who resisted all of these invitations to deceit and has remained honest.

When you do tell lies, people tend not to trust you and may start to disbelieve what you say, even when it is completely true. There may be times when you really want others to take you seriously and believe you. Then what? Lying can destroy intimate relationships, close friendships and even work relationships. When you can't trust someone, how can you be close? It isn't possible. The lies stand as barriers that tell loved ones, "I don't care enough about you to really let you into my world."

Lack of authenticity breeds distrust and disrespect. When you are in the habit of lying, you start to think everyone else is lying. Lying hurts the people you lie to, especially those you are close to, those who really value you and want to feel valued by you. If you end up a chronic liar, your ability to love and be loved becomes impacted. You get a reputation as a person lacking in integrity, someone not to be trusted. *Satya,* deep honesty without harm to others can heal this tendency with practice. So if this is your issue, pick yourself up, brush yourself off and try again to find your integrity and live in truth.

Getting Real and Being Yourself

Applying *Satya,* compassionate honesty or even *rita,* literal truthfulness, to yourself is freeing. Self-honesty is extremely important in being able to evaluate your own motives and to understand your own actions. When you are not established in self-honesty, then the integrity of your actions becomes compromised since you cannot see clearly the layers of intent in the mind. Those actions done with *sattvic* (pure) life-supporting intentions, service to living beings and the Divine, are forthright and sincere. However, sometimes underneath good intentions, other intentions can be harbored in the mind, such as personal gain. Even *tamasic* (stagnant), static or stuck intentions of resentment or anger may come forward subtly in your actions. If you have not worked on self-honesty, you may not be able to see these more covert intentions. When you cannot see them, you become susceptible to being ruled by them.

If you hide who and what you are by always saying what others want, never being honest with yourself, never being truthful, what happens? You get in the habit of deceiving others and then you begin to believe the deception yourself. This delusion about self can grow and grow until you do not have clear, clean relationships between thought, word and deed. Disturbances grow in the mind. The mind becomes slippery, agitated and restless. Anxiety and even depression may result from being disconnected from authenticity.

Your ability to express yourself diminishes because you are not expressing the truth of yourself. Your expression in the world becomes muted. In the *So be honestly* mind, the backlash of energy causes *true to who you* distortions in your thinking and *are, authentic.* self-deception. Much time and personal potential can be lost in this type of cycle. *Satya* allows the thoughts in your mind, your words and your deeds to be one. So be honestly true to who you are, authentic.

The Slippery Slope of Satya

As has been said, *Satya* is not literal truth but the use of words with honesty and a sense of benevolence. Its base is in the indivisible nature of truth and love. In the practical application of *Satya*, there may be times when we need to withhold information in order not to hurt someone, such as when having to find the right time to tell someone that he or she has lost a job. Or we may even find, in an extreme situation, a need to lie to protect someone or save them from harm or trauma, such as when in a car accident a partner is killed and the survivor is in critical condition and may die from the shock if told straight out of her loved one's demise.

However if we do not know ourselves well and lack stark self-honesty, we may begin to misuse these elements of *Satya*, not fostering benevolence with our withholding or misrepresentations but rather our personal beliefs and self-interests. We may begin to feel from time to time that it is in everyone's best interest if we lie just a bit when, in reality, it is in our own interest. We find ourselves in the quagmire of self-delusion not able to distinguish the truth from our own self-created fantasies. This path leads down a road to ignorance and suffering.

To avoid this slippery slope, it is important to live in integrity with yourself and the Divine within you. Living in integrity involves a clear sense of conscience, being honest and forthright, and applying that straight-forwardness and clear thinking with kind and caring intentions. Making the person you are within the same person you present to the world around you is living with *LIVING IN INTEGRITY INVOLVES A CLEAR SENSE OF CONSCIENCE.* real integrity. To do this you need to know yourself. So be ever mindful. Strive to be self-aware and know your own motives. Let not the veil of ignorance obscure the truth and lead you down the road of self-deception. Let the rudder of loving kindness guide you to the depths of truth within you.

Compassion and Truth

When you are following *Ahimsa* as well as *Satya* and have compassion, you see the faults and failings of others and of yourself honestly, and you accept them as part of our shared humanity. When you have love as well as honesty, in that loving kindness you can accept human frailties and weaknesses even in yourself, not necessarily support them, but accept them. When you begin to evaluate yourself honestly, you begin to see parts that you may not like to see, motivations, subtle intentions and actions that you would not like to admit to yourself and cannot accept in yourself or

43

in others. This is where honesty and compassion meet the challenge of your own self-judgments. It is easy to run, go into denial and from anger and self-hatred resort to harmful habits and addictions. It is much more challenging to stay with truth and learn unconditional love.

For meditation to go deep and lead to self-realization, authentic self-analysis and self-evaluation are essential. You need to be able to see the multiple layers of motivation that play in the mind and get acted out in the world. This ability to perceive the subtleties of intention and motive gives you clarity of mind. From this clarity, based in self-revealing truthfulness, you begin to be able to distinguish that which leads toward the divine Self and that which leads away.

THE KEY TO LOVING OTHERS IS TO LOVE ONESELF.

This quality of discrimination is born of honesty, but truthfulness alone will not give you the full scope. In addition to self-honesty there needs to be the desire to do no harm, compassion for living beings. *Ahimsa* is needed in combination with truthfulness to develop true discrimination. The key is to love others and to love yourself. Develop a clear mind through the practice of *Satya* and compassionate love for all beings. Then the deep love required to know truth and to discriminate the real from the unreal will unfold.

Living in Reality

When you adhere to *Satya,* you speak with the intent to enhance the life of others. You do not speak with ill intent. When people become established in the practice of *Satya,* their words become the very embodiment of the compassionate love of the Divine. They begin to move in harmony with the divine flow. When this happens, whatever they say comes true. Do you know why? Do you think it is that they have the occult power to make things happen as they wish? This is not the reason.

The words that are said become truth because the person is so deeply ensconced in the loving compassion of the Divine and in the truth that underlies all love that they cannot utter anything that is not in harmony with the universe. Therefore, what is said becomes an expression of the divine flow. It becomes a fact and will occur because the person cannot express anything other than the truth.

This is what happens when a person follows *Satya* fully. He or she learns real truthfulness and also acquires a deep sense of discrimination. When you learn to speak truth, to think truth not in literal words of precision but in harmony with the essential nature of all beings, then you come closer and closer to reality. You begin to acquire the ability to discriminate between what is truth and what is illusion. You develop the capacity for *viveka* or discrimination between the real and the unreal and finally merge with the deep truth.

ACQUIRE THE ABILITY TO DISCRIMINATE BETWEEN WHAT IS TRUTH AND WHAT IS ILLUSION.

Ultimate Truth

Sat is the Sanskrit word for the deep truth that lies at the core of all existence. The process of discovering this truth entails discriminative reflection on the nature of what is. Gaining insight into the nature of truth ultimately leads to the core of

Satya; that is pure love, pure consciousness and pure being. This is the one eternal Self, the ocean that has no shore. It is the point of singularity at the very center of the universe, the unmanifest essence from which all creation emerges and unto which it returns. This is *Sat*, the essence of *Satya*. It is the deep truth underlying all else, the Self of yourself, the core of your being.

When you connect with truth, it will ultimately lead you to these timeless shores. As you go deeper and deeper into self-honesty, you become the embodiment of truth; you become the hollow reed, the empty container through which the winds of eternity play in the halls of creation.

Satya, like the other practices of *Yama* and *Niyama*, is not an idle practice to make you appear to others to be a good person. Rather, it develops the mind so that you can comprehend the nature of infinite consciousness. Otherwise your mind is so consumed in distortions of reality that there is no ability to perceive divinity. To be able to perceive that which is subtle, that which is the underlying harmony within the universe, you need to have the capacity for subtle perception. When you are practicing *Yama* and *Niyama*, perception becomes subtler and your sense of discrimination grows, the sense of love grows and clarity ensues.

Asteya
Non-Stealing

Asteya is the yogic practice of avoiding taking what does not belong to you or is not freely offered to you. It includes greedy desires expressing in our thoughts, words and deeds. There are many reasons we may covet what we do not have and be jealous, feeling someone else has more than we do. Maybe they have success, money, popularity, health, power, a good job, a partner we wish we had, or even spiritual experiences we want to have. Whatever it is we feel another has and we wish was ours instead of theirs comes from a sense of lack within ourselves, a feeling that we are not enough as we are.

The desire to take from others is inherently rooted in our own sense of inadequacy as well as discontent with ourselves and what life has given us. We feel disempowered and unable to manifest what we feel we need in life. From this sense of personal disempowerment comes the need to acquire whatever it is we feel we need from outside of ourselves. We begin to resent people who have things we do not have and begin to feel justified in taking them. This can lead to actual theft, not only of property but also of ideas, relationships and even identity. If not actual theft, it leads to jealousy and avarice. And this leads to more unhappiness and discontent with ourselves and with our lives in general.

So goes the downward spiral of low self-worth, discontent, disempowerment, resentment, anger, jealousy, and greed. This leads to more of a sense of lack and finally bitterness, resentment and despair. It is not the yogic way, nor is it the way to a sense of well-being. Even the rich may wish for what they do not have and then live in miserable discontent as a result. Those who are successful thieves may glory in their success for a time but as they continue to take from others, they begin to feel very afraid of others taking from them. They build walls of distrust with all and barricade themselves behind their own growing fears, dishonesty and ruthless attitudes. They do not walk a path toward happiness or psychological health.

So the *yogis* of ancient times warned against following this self-destructive path, encouraging us to be honest, do no harm and not covet what others have. Believing in yourself, feeling contentment and enjoyment of your life, however simple it may be, is the path to self-empowerment. It brings the realization that you can make your own life beautiful on your own. By developing positive attitudes, generosity of heart and mind, and seeing what is good about our own lives we become content and thus happy. Rather than living in the shadow of feeling inadequate that makes us somehow less than someone else who has something we do not, we move toward well-being and wholeness. This is part of *dharma*, the way toward the one eternal Self.

The Hungry Ghost

Avoiding the desire to have what belongs to others is significant when you want to know God. That desire leads to taking what you want, which only increases your discontent. First, something small is stolen and it doesn't seem to be a problem. Then something larger is stolen and again there seems to be no problem. So then more is stolen and soon all sense of boundary is lost. You become ruled by discontent and desire. Coveting what others have and taking from them feeds the hungry ghost that cannot be satisfied. You feed it and you feed it and it only grows hungrier. It is better to be content with what is. When the hungry ghost of restless desire is not fed, then the desires begin to subside and peace of mind has an opportunity to arise.

Most people who are sincerely seeking spiritual life are generally not thieves. However the attitudes that create mental theft are encouraged not only by our individual circumstances but also by our culture. We live in a materialistic society. What is the mantra of capitalism? Want more! Buy more! Acquire more! Have more than everyone else! When someone else has something you don't have, you are encouraged to acquire it. However, this attitude is fundamentally a violation of *Asteya*. There is no *COVETING WHAT OTHERS HAVE AND TAKING FROM THEM FEEDS THE HUNGRY GHOST THAT CANNOT BE SATISFIED.* contentment in a mind that always needs to acquire more and desires that which someone else has. It is the psychology of a hungry ghost.

In one form or another, suffering comes to all in this world. The person who lives in poverty looks to the rich and says, "Look what they have. Their life is good. If only I had that money, I would be happy too. I could have all that I want." In this way, a person imagines so much happiness in the rich person, coveting the wealth. The individual lives in misery, always wanting, thinking, "If only I had that money, that car, that nice house, then I would be happy."

Meanwhile, the person with the nice car and house has just lost a wife, a husband or the love of a child and is crying himself or herself to sleep. The wealthy person is not necessarily happy. He or she may well be longing for a simple life, yearning for the love of children or for the wife to be back home again. The person may be wishing just as intently and with the same restlessness as the poor person for a happy life. Highs and lows are part and parcel of every person's life. Never think you are alone in your suffering. Even those you think have everything you want may be very unhappy. So why covet what another has? It may not buy you the happiness you imagine it would.

Real Need

When exploring *Asteya*, one cannot help but think of situations of extreme poverty and deprivation where basic survival needs are not met – war-torn lawless lands, corrupt governments, harsh dictatorships and abject poverty where people are truly starving. This is not the case for most of us where our desires to acquire what others have arise from our personal discontent and attitudes toward life.

In these situations where extreme oppression and starvation exist, do not those starving people long for food that others have or even the opportunity for a bath or medical care? Do they not dream of having what they so desperately need and even feel terrible anger and resentment toward those who live in comfort and keep them oppressed? When society is out of balance, people cannot be expected not to resent oppressors. However, this is not the same as violating *Asteya* by coveting what others have. These desires arise as a result of injustice and abject need.

WHEN SOCIETY IS OUT OF BALANCE, PEOPLE CANNOT BE EXPECTED NOT TO RESENT OPPRESSORS.

The love of the human heart demands to be seen and respected. Every creature loves its life from the small bird to the great elephant. They all want to be able to survive, flourish and find happiness. When extreme imbalances in the social fabric lead to deprivation, then how can people contemplate their relation to God? First and foremost they must be fed and their basic needs attended to. Then they can contemplate their motives. *Asteya* encourages us not to take what is not ours but everyone has a right to have the basic needs met, not to starve, not to be slaughtered like sheep, to have their humanity acknowledged. To desire this is not a violation of *Asteya*. It is to affirm life.

Integration

If you want happiness, lead a simple life having only what you need and stop storing your hopes in material objects or the idea of possessing something you do not have. For your own well-being, learn to be content in yourself. When you finally let go of your restless desires, the tendency to wish to take from another dissipates. Your mind becomes quiet.

Learn to see everything as the expression of the infinite *Brahma* and to direct all your desires to the Divine Consciousness, which is expressing through those objects. *Asteya* supports being content with what you have. Though your life may be simple, when following *Asteya* you are living within your means not coveting what belongs to others, not thinking how you are going to get something you do not have. You have learned to be content with what you have and who you are, with what life has allotted to you and to find happiness within your own life and your own means. The hungry ghost of desire is not fed and so begins to fade from your life. Then you can be truly happy with yourself and focus on what is good about your life.

Brahmacharya
Transmuting the Desire Mind

"I shut not my eyes; I close not my ears,
I do not mortify my body:
I see with eyes open and
Behold His beauty everywhere..."
SONGS OF KABIR BY TAGORE

The next aspect of the practice of *Yama* is *Brahmacharya*. In Sanskrit, *Brahmacharya* blends two words, *Brahma* (God) and *charya* (to follow). This practice involves seeing everything in this universe as the manifestation of the *Brahma*, the primal source of being. It does not simply mean to be celibate. Although the idea of celibacy and restraint is often associated with *Brahmacharya*, it is not actually the deepest interpretation. Though, for certain spiritual purposes celibacy may be beneficial, in the deeper understanding of *Brahmacharya*, one sees all desires of the body and mind as manifestations of the desire for the one true divine Self. Thus you dedicate all desires to *Brahma*, the primordial Self of all beings.

SEE EVERYTHING IN THIS UNIVERSE AS THE MANIFESTATION OF THE BRAHMA, THE PRIMAL SOURCE OF BEING.

This practice is based on the fundamental knowledge that all existence is composed of one eternal, unending, Self-aware consciousness. Each and every object in this universe from a blade of grass to a mountain is in its essence composed of this primordial consciousness. All beings long for and desire to return to this state of wholeness where lasting happiness and true fulfillment abide.

Yet living in this temporal world of forms and colors, we become forgetful of this source. Our restless yearning for our eternal Self gets attached to different forms and experiences in the world that we hope will make us happy. However, all things change and that which brings us happiness today becomes the source of our suffering tomorrow when our circumstances change. We fail to see that what attracts us in the forms we cling to is, in fact, the essential nature of all that is, the infinite primordial Self. We fail to recognize that all forms are composed of the Divine.

We forget that it is the eternal *Brahma* for which we long. *Brahmacharya* is a practice of remembrance of what we really long for in all of our desires.

Celibacy and Sublimation of Desire
In truth *Brahmacharya* is a process of sublimating our desires for sex, power, material objects, approval, name and fame into love for God. Within each of us is a restlessness born of our identity with our bodymind ego structure. This identity is based in ignorance of our true unified nature that is one with the eternal source of being. From this small ego and body-based identity, we assume out of ignorance *(avidya)* that we are small and separate. From this comes a need to acquire things in order to be safe, survive and find happiness, and we fear anything and everything that may interfere with our survival, especially death. There is a restless need but, in reality, it is not for any external form. Our need is to return to grace, return to the wholeness of our essential nature.

In ignorance and suffering we seek that which may alleviate our pain and thus enter into the world of desires. However, the fulfillment of our desires only gives us temporary pleasure or happiness as the joys of this world are fleeting. It is when we sublimate these desires to a deeper wisdom that this externalizing our energy into desire is transmuted into the awakening of our real nature.

The true celibacy of *Brahmacharya* is the renunciation of our ignorance. It is a vow to avoid indulging in the depletion of our life force by chasing desires for forms and, instead, to recognize the one true Self we are truly seeking. The practice of *Brahmacharya* does not require that you abstain from physical love unless you have chosen renunciation. If it did and was followed, the world would pass away because no one would have children. It is not against *Brahmacharya* to be a householder or family person.

However, how you direct your thoughts determines whether your actions are within the scope of *Brahmacharya*. For example, if you are continually thinking about sex, you are not practicing *Brahmacharya*. Yet if you are thinking of the Goddess, and she comes before you in the form of your wife and you unite, then this love becomes a sacred communion that directs the desires of the body and mind toward the one eternal Self. When you lust for another person for your own pleasure, you have lost the practice of *Brahmacharya* but when you see the Divine in another and love your divine Beloved in manifest form, then your mind

OUR NEED IS TO RETURN TO GRACE, RETURN TO THE WHOLENESS OF OUR ESSENTIAL NATURE.

dwells on the infinite *Brahma*. Maintaining this ideation, directing the passions of the body and mind to the one eternal Self, *Brahmacharya* is followed.

Everything and everyone is a manifestation of the Divine. Direct all passions toward the Divine. Then this world of earthly forms becomes a heaven on earth.

Seeing the Divine Everywhere

It is best to transmute passions of the mind and body into a connection to your primordial Source. For example, when you see a particularly beautiful flower, you may feel drawn to it. When you see it as a flower separate from yourself, as something you want to acquire, this awakens desires. However when you see the beautiful *YOU RECOGNIZE THAT IT IS THE ONE ETERNAL SELF YOU ARE DRAWN TO.*
flower, not as an object separate from yourself, but as infinite divine consciousness manifesting in the beauty of the lovely flower, you are practicing *Brahmacharya*. You recognize that it is the one eternal Self you are drawn to. This understanding arises when you practice *Brahmacharya*.

The same is true for all desires, all lusts of the body and the mind. Without this practice there will always be distortion in the mind. The practice of *Brahmacharya* clarifies the mind and leads to *viveka*, true discrimination and the wisdom to know the unreal from the real. Purity of heart and mind result from this practice. To see all as the Divine is to become established in a deep knowledge of the truth and to cultivate God-realization.

Practiced in its crudest form, *Brahmacharya* is simply not

overindulging in desires. This may include abstaining from overeating or excess sexual activity, avoiding gambling or unnecessary shopping, basically not getting wrapped up in your cravings. It does not involve suppressing your desires or denying them. It is more a matter of taming the cravings within you and refraining from excess, not letting them govern you.

However practiced in the subtle sphere, *Brahmacharya* involves seeing within all of your desires a deep longing for the Divine, a longing to return to wholeness and unconditional love. In this subtle practice, you attribute your love of sweets, your desire for a brownie, to longing for the sweetness of the Divine. Knowledge of divine beauty and the ocean of divine love is sweet knowledge. You begin to realize that you want this sweet knowledge. Your desire for your sweet brownie is but an expression of this profound longing for connection to Love Divine. The sweetness is an aspect of the Divine Consciousness that expresses in all forms. Do you see? It is to see the Divine in all that exists. This is sweet knowledge indeed.

Clear thinking results when *Brahmacharya* is practiced along with *Ahimsa* and *Satya*. Then there is both compassion and discrimination. The more you practice, the more subtle your understanding becomes. When you adhere to these practices, you maintain balance. By practicing harmlessness, living in integrity, avoiding overindulging, seeing everything as the manifestation of the Divine, and directing all passions toward the one infinite Self of yourself, this world becomes sweet indeed.

Aparigraha
Simplicity and Generosity

The final practice of *Yama*, the yogic avoidances, is *Aparigraha*, to avoid accumulating beyond your needs. It literally means not to grasp, hoard, hold on to things or take more than you need. It encourages a life of simplicity and generosity on all levels, having what is truly necessary and no more.

Less is More

This practice encourages you not to accumulate excessive material objects as the mind becomes engrossed in and bound by material objects when you do. Having more than you need does not usually lead to satisfaction but, instead, to an increased desire to acquire more and more. Perhaps you have rightly earned what you

HAVING MORE THAN YOU NEED DOES NOT USUALLY LEAD TO SATISFACTION

have; you have not stolen, but still – like the thief who does not follow *Asteya* – your desire is to grasp the objects, to covet the objects and to acquire more. This attitude makes the mind as well as the environment cluttered. It clutters the mind with desire. In addition, what you have gotten in excess will no doubt leave another with less than he or she is due. A kind of imbalance occurs in your life and mental balance cannot be maintained in this circumstance.

Living a Simple Life

To follow *Aparigraha*, you do not need to sell all that you own and only own the shirt on your back. You need to meet your needs and, depending upon your situation, your needs will vary. For one who is a simple ascetic or monk, perhaps only a begging bowl and a change of clothes is needed. That may be the path of *Aparigraha* for an ascetic or *sadhu*.

However for someone with a family and children to rear in modern western society, probably a little more is needed. You might need an apartment or house to live in, transportation for work and school, books to educate your children, even the money for their college education. You will need food for your family and a refrigerator to keep it cool. You will even need a stove to cook meals and dishes to eat on. You require a certain amount of possessions to maintain the life of a family person. This is natural. However, you do not need to have three cars. You do not need to store huge amounts of money in the bank coveting it for yourself. You do not need twenty pairs of shoes, or closets and rooms full of thing you do not use or unnecessary luxuries.

If you accumulate beyond your needs, the practice of *Aparigraha* is lost. Then the house becomes filled with an accumulation of so many things you don't need. These things become a clutter in the *THIS HABIT OF ACQUISITION* environment and then where *IS THE PATH TO HELL.* is your cleanliness in your cluttered environment? It is better not to covet, not to desire what belongs to another and it is better not to accumulate what you do not need. Have what you need. Take what you need for yourself, for your own family, for your basic wants. However, when you accumulate beyond your needs, it leaves the mind cluttered and it also instills fear.

Do you know why you have accumulated all of these objects around you? You have so many objects and yet you go on accumulating, accumulating. Though you do not need them, still you accumulate and why? Because it makes you feel safe. You begin to feel, "These objects will make me safe; they will save me in the end. As long as I have so much money in the bank, as long as I have so many houses, as long as I have so many books, as long as I have so much of this and so much of that, I will be safe, my life will be secure. I will know who I am. I will know what I have. I will be safe." In this way, you place your welfare in material objects and not in the divine Self. This ideation does not work. It will not buy you permanent safety; it will only buy you suffering.

This habit of acquisition is the path to hell. True safety can only be found in the Divine. No other shelter will be with you when you are old and feeble. When your time to depart the physical world comes, there is no other shelter for you. You will not be able to take all of these objects with you. So do not make them your shelter. It will only cause you suffering. Have only what you need for a good life. This is appropriate and is the maxim of *Aparigraha*.

Fear and Safety

What is most significant about *Aparigraha* is the impact it has upon our minds. It is fear that drives us to accumulate material objects and other types of possessions in the hope of warding off suffering. We hope our amassed wealth will keep us safe, protected from life's difficulties but, in reality, the material wealth is like the house of straw that will blow away when the going gets really rough. You can't take this wealth with you in the end. Like the house of stone built on solid rock, spiritual truth or *vidya*, the deep truth of our eternal nature is the real safe harbor in the storm of life. This base is lasting, enduring in even the worst situations. It will carry you even beyond the veil of this worldly life.

Rather than spending all our time and life-force energy accumulating material security, when we place our trust in divine essence and work to know the Self, the rewards are far more lasting and effective. The practice of *Aparigraha* allows us to separate our security and well-being from how much we own or can possess. It allows space from our tendencies to amass things around us. As a result, we can think clearly and begin to place our welfare where it really belongs, in knowing our own Self and the ocean of divinity at our source. This is the real shelter in the storm.

We can build our houses of straw not only of material objects and wealth but anything we tend to want to possess more and more of in order to secure our well-being. This can be name and fame, power, prestige or whatever we try to amass to make us safe, important or somehow immune to the trials and tribulations of life.

Simplicity

We live in a society where a few have much wealth and many go without even their most basic needs being met. If you sit on excess wealth when others are in hunger and in pain, how can you realize God? How can you know the one Self? For the divine Self lies equally in all. Knowing this, can one part of the Self accumulate more and more while another part has so little? Rather than accumulating more, perhaps it is better to use wealth in service to living beings. Excess accumulation of wealth not only harms you by misdirecting your trust and energy but harms others as well, for when excess material wealth lies in the hands of a few it creates a lack of needed resources among others.

When you do not follow *Aparigraha,* when you begin holding on to material possessions or whatever else you have put your faith in to shield you from life's struggles, the accumulation makes a cluttered house, a cluttered mind and a cluttered life. Those do not bode well for meditation upon the Great. That is why the *yogis* say

IT IS BETTER TO USE WEALTH IN SERVICE TO LIVING BEINGS.

to live a simple life, to lead a life based on the solid ground of being and in the love that weaves all living beings into one interdependent, interwoven community. Put your trust in your divine Source rather than what you can accumulate.

CHAPTER III

Living Your Truth

Niyama

The practices of *Niyama* are essential elements of a spiritual life. These practices are fundamental to be able to move toward the realization of divine consciousness. They facilitate personal development so that knowledge of the Divine may shine like a bright light within the mind.

Niyama is essential to follow for a person to become a true man or woman of wisdom. Basic to spiritual life, the practices of *Niyama* are helpful for everyone. Be you a beginning meditator or the most advanced yogi, do your best to follow these tenets if you want to know God.

The purpose of the *Niyama* practices is to focus the mind on the eternal source of all being

THE DIVINE CANNOT BE HELD IN THE MIND OF A HUMAN BEING.

and to prepare the mind so that divine consciousness may be known. Without some form of the practices that are outlined in *Niyama*, the image of the Divine cannot be held in the mind of a human being. It will waver; it will distort; it will not be seen clearly.

These are not secondary practices; they are primary

practices. They must be done for a person to have knowledge of the Infinite. This is not a rule that you must follow to be a good person. It is not a moral code, in that sense. It is a practical analysis of what is necessary to transform the mind so that subtle perception may be acquired and Divinity may be perceived.

Saucha
Purity of Body and Mind

Saucha is the yogic practice of purification of the body and the mind. To practice it is to clean away all the dirt that may clutter the mind so that perception of the Infinite is possible. In this purification of the mind, like the cleaning of a window, there are specific actions that may be taken. The mind has many layers. The outermost layer of the mind is the physical body that resides in this physical world. Therefore, one needs to purify the body as well as the conscious mind and the subconscious mind. All the layers of the mind must be purified. The first and most basic action one can take to purify the mind is to keep the body and surrounding environment clean.

External Purity
When the body and the room are kept clean and all that you come in contact with is cared for with reverence, the process of purifying the mind is enhanced. Thus, the first step to developing *Saucha* is keeping the body pure. Keep the hair clean and the body well washed, fresh and sweet smelling.

Do practices to purify the body internally as well. Fasting several times a month to allow the body to rest, drinking water to clean the body internally and doing similar practices that heal and purify the body will help create a pure subtle vehicle for spiritual awakening.

Treat all objects in the environment with reverence and care to bring your mind to a state of purity. When you keep order in your environment, take care of the objects and beings around you, it changes your attitude toward life. Be careful in your treatment of all objects and beings in your sphere. When you keep your environment clean and your *PURIFY THE BODY TO HELP CREATE A PURE SUBTLE VEHICLE FOR SPIRITUAL AWAKENING.* body clean, it creates a mentality of attentiveness. You learn to attend to your environment and to all in it with subtlety and awareness. In contrast, when your environment is sloppy or you are disheveled there is less attentiveness. Through the practice of *Saucha*, you grow your capacity to attend with subtlety and sentience and to create sentience in your environment and your person.

Internal Purity

The practice of *Saucha* does not end with taking care of your body and your environment. Keeping the body pure and the environment clean is part and parcel of spiritual practice but beyond the physical is the psychic realm where purity and cleanliness of mind is the real work. In addition to the outer practices of cleanliness and purity, there are the inner practices in the mental sphere. The mind needs to be kept free from impurities. When your mind is clouded like a dirty window, you cannot see through it to the treasures held within. When you clean the window, making it so clear that not one drop of dirt exists, then that which is on the other side of the window becomes crystal clear to you. It is as if the window has become nonexistent altogether.

A pure mind is a clean mind, a clear mind devoid of mess and debris. How does one purify the mind? We know that water will purify the external body and good eating and drinking habits will purify the internal body. But what purifies the mind? When you care for your physical body and for your environment, they become pure, clean vessels. The mind can be purified in a clean vessel by doing *Brahma sadhana,* meditation upon the Divine, and by maintaining pure thoughts. When you concentrate on the Divine and learn to look on the bright side of life, your entire attitude toward yourself changes.

A Positive Attitude

Stress is a big problem in the world today. Although people are stressed by many different situations, much stress is self-made. When you want to solve your stress, it is helpful to learn to cultivate positive thought patterns. Learn to love yourself and appreciate what you have. Learn to feel that *LEARN TO FEEL GRACE IS IN EVERY MOMENT OF YOUR LIFE.* grace is in every moment of your life and know that all that you have is given by grace. Be happy with who you are. Find the joy. Find the goodness and the brightness. Find your peace with what is and then in that brightness, that contentment, come to equanimity where the mind settles and acceptance, love and peace ensue.

Peacefulness, *Santosha,* combined with purity of heart and mind, *Saucha,* together form the clear waters. With these practices, your meditation becomes clear and you can see to the depths. There is neither disturbance nor haze in the waters of the mind. The waters are clean and pure, quiet, serene and thus the depths of your being become visible.

However, when you are wrapped up in yourself, involved in self-centeredness, even though the mind can be made pure and clear and calm, the self-absorption in your own ego becomes a barrier. The sense of duality, the sense of the importance of your own fears and needs become so great that you focus on your involvement in the personal, in the acquisition of what is needed for your individual ego-self. Then the divine Self becomes obscured. When the body is kept pure, when the environment is cared for with attentiveness, then slowly, slowly it affects the attitudes within the mind and the ego-oriented focus lessens. A new attitude begins to dawn, an attitude of reverence for all life. This reverence for life brings about a feeling of purity in the mind. The heart becomes pure.

The practice that is most helpful in purifying the mind is to disengage the mind from impure and degenerative thoughts. This is not so easily done but as you continue to treat all objects and all beings with reverence and care, then the mind begins to adopt the attitude that everything is the form of *Brahma,* the primordial eternal Divinity. As discussed in *Brahmacharya,* care for everyone and everything with utmost reverence. Know that you cannot exploit anyone or anything, as all is the manifestation of the one true primordial Self.

This is a pure thought. It brings the mind to a state of cleanliness, a state of inner purity in which the reflection of the infinite consciousness may become bright. A pure mind can perceive the Infinite

A PURE MIND CAN PERCEIVE
THE INFINITE.

because it is not filled with the dirt of selfishness, the dirt of greed, the dirt of lust. It is not filled with mental desires that promote a small ego. It is filled instead with sweet and careful thoughts that treat all objects and all beings with reverence and think upon everyone and everything with love.

To cultivate this attitude, practice replacing negative tendencies with their opposites. For example, when there is a tendency to become angry or hostile toward others, then consciously cultivate polite, sweet and smiling behavior. It is not that expressing anger is bad. You may get angry at times but intentionally cultivate the opposite behavior to quell the mind, to gain equanimity, and to clean the surface of the mind of all of the imbalances. A balanced mind is a clean mind, a pure mind. A pure mind holds reverence for all objects and all beings and for self, because a pure mind holds a pure reflection of the cosmic awareness.

In the clear mind, the divine unitary essence of all things is easily seen because the waters of the mind become completely clear, still and transparent. When one has this cleanliness of mind, this purity of thought, then it is easy to know the eternal Self and for the mind to have equanimity. Equanimity is balance in the mind. A pure mind is a balanced mind that fosters purity in one's thoughts.

When the mind becomes balanced, one attains the state of equanimity; one attains peace of mind. With *Saucha*, purity of mind develops through actions that remove the impurities and wash the dirt from the lens of the mind. To develop equanimity, first of all *Saucha* needs to be cultivated. Then peace of mind may emerge. This peace or equanimity is called *Santosha*, the second aspect of the practice of *Niyama*.

Santosha
Serenity and Equanimity

Santosha, equanimity of mind, comes through letting go, through acceptance. It is not an avoidance of the conflicts or the struggles in life. On the contrary, equanimity comes when a person can find deep contentment, deep acceptance in the midst of conflict or struggle. Real peace comes not through avoidance but through mental equilibrium in all situations and circumstances.

Bring all pleasant and unpleasant experiences into equanimity by recognizing that all things of this world are temporal. Do not feed the negative experiences in life with your anticipation, worry and distress. Instead cultivate equanimity and positive thoughts and emotions. Then in time, the mind settles down. It gains peace and calm and is more suited for meditative practice.

TO BE FREE IS TO ACCEPT LIGHT AND SHADOW.

Self-Acceptance

It is hard to find contentment in life when you cannot accept yourself. There is a layer of subtlety that can be developed where you become discriminative, clear-minded and perceive people's intentions, including your own. This is when you become free, when you can see not only other people's shadows but your own shadows. Look straight into them and see just as clearly as in the light without response, reaction, or rejection. As long as you reject the parts of yourself that are shadowy, you will not be the master of them. When you can love and accept all parts of yourself, you can love all parts of others, and the play of shadow and light becomes just a play in consciousness. You do not struggle to acquire one state and reject another; this struggle is the human condition of bondage.

To be free is to accept light and shadow, joy and struggle, and to truly accept yourself as is, with your strengths and your weaknesses. Life is complex, never black and white, never all good or all bad. It is a mix and each one of us is a mix also. When you learn to stop running and to be with what is, even learn to love what is, then life unfolds. The shadow loses its hold and you become free to choose, to be. All of your energy is not taken up defending against the parts of yourself you cannot accept or love. Find the Divine even in your pain, your hurt and your wounds and be ever so loving to that wounded person within you. Then you can learn truly to love others. This self-love and self-acceptance is the key to psychological maturity and to an awakening vision of the Divine. Where then does the Divine not abide?

Being In the World but Not of It

Some people think that if they remove themselves from worldly disturbances then they can attain serenity or peace of mind. A hermit cloistered in a monastery or alone in a cave may think he has found equanimity, that he understands peace of mind, but let him go into the city, in the middle of the bazaar, and attempt to purchase a bangle. The shop owner haggles with him on the price and the crowds are bumping and pushing on him. The noise and dust is all-around and a man gets angry with him for some minor offense. Then let the hermit see whether he has attained equanimity and peace of mind.

Even in such circumstances, a person who has true equanimity will be unperturbed. He may yell back at the man; he may haggle with the shop owner but his equipoise will be unaffected. For when the mind has sunk deep into the ocean of *Brahma*, there comes a contentment that no circumstance can disturb. There comes a peace that is abiding, eternal.

To develop this equilibrium one needs to avoid becoming overly impassioned for material objects. When one desires money and then a little money comes in, is the desire satisfied? No. The person then wants more money. If he becomes a millionaire then he wants to be a multimillionaire. A little is never enough. Even when a whole lot is there, then still it is not enough, as this craving of the mind becomes so great. To attain equanimity, this tendency of the mind to be overly absorbed with passions for material objects must be curbed.

Emotions rise and fall. So today you are happy and tomorrow you are angry or disturbed by someone's actions. The next day you feel sad and lonely. The following day you are nervous and the day after that you feel good again. Emotions are like this. They are fickle and they may go this way and that. One cannot rely on feelings alone to recognize the Divine. One must utilize one's mind as well and one's subtle perceptions. Feelings are like thoughts in the mind. They go here and there following different streams and you should treat them in the same fashion.

Pay attention only to knowledge of the eternal Divinity, the experience of the eternal Self, and the *sattvic* emotions that arise from that experience. Do not be overly concerned with the other thoughts in the mind and feelings that rise and fall. Let them come and go. Many feelings, thoughts, experiences of pain and sorrow, loss, nervousness and fear come in the human life. When one accepts them all as the ever-changing faces of the Divine, as the Beloved speaking to you through different experiences, then they will have no hold on you.

When you are in reaction to certain types of experiences, resisting them and attempting to avoid the accompanying feelings, the reaction sustains your attachment. You attach to the elimination of unwanted feelings and as a result you draw them closer to you. For example, when you are grieving the loss of a loved one and you resist the experience or try to suppress it, the grief tends to linger. It remains unresolved because you have not accepted it or come to peace with it. When you ease your mind with acceptance, contentment and equanimity then whatever the feelings or thoughts rising and falling within, you integrate them and maintain the long view. Today they are this way. Tomorrow they will be another way. With this approach your experiences are less distressing. Then, when the final days of life come, the experiences will not cling to you. They will roll off like the water off a duck's back because you have not latched onto them.

Settling the Passions

When you do not practice *Yama* and *Niyama*, your mind is turbulent. Then all through your meditation, the turbulence of your mind is churning and you can do nothing but think of all the weals and woes of your life. When you do not detach from these passions, you are ever concerned about your problems. They fill the mind. The beginning meditator and even the more experienced meditator that gets distracted may have a great deal of trouble with such thoughts in the mind. Additionally, one may have trouble in meditation with awareness of different physical problems. Some find that they cannot sit. It causes this and that pain and spoils concentration. They are sensitive to sounds around them or in the distance. A dog barks. Someone has a television in the next apartment. They are hyper aware of every little tiny disturbance.

HOW MAY ONE WITHDRAW THE MIND FROM THESE PASSIONS?

To meditate, the mind must be somehow withdrawn from these passions and discomforts. Now, you may wonder, how is this done? How may one withdraw the mind from these passions that engross the mind so that it is thrown here and thrown there on the waves of this created existence? How does one remove oneself from these tortuous desires? The method is a simple one; it is through self-reflection, becoming aware that you are not this passion for money. You are not this need for fulfillment. You are not these passions and needs that you feel. They are expressions of the mind but you are not those expressions.

Make some mental distance between you and your passions and needs. Then ascribe divinity to every object of this universe. Think, "It is not the money I am truly desiring. It is the infinite happiness that I mistakenly thought perhaps money would gain for me." In this way curb your desires. Do not attempt to suppress them for they will only pop out in a different form. Instead, attribute godhood to them. Perceive the essential nature of all that is around you; make the mind pure through the practice of *Saucha*. Make it content with the practice of *Santosha*; develop equanimity of mind.

THE FETTERS OF THE MIND BECOME THINNED AND FINALLY BROKEN ALTOGETHER AND THE PERSON ATTAINS EQUANIMITY.

Do you know what happens when the mind begins to settle from all of these passions, pulls, needs and desires? Once it begins to settle a little, then you gain the ability to reflect on your own existence and realize that you are connected to all beings. You begin to realize that you are neither inferior nor superior to anyone. You realize that you are a child of the Infinite. You are divine. You are great and all beings are great. This entire cosmos is the manifestation of the Divine.

When equanimity of mind occurs through knowledge of the Infinite, ascribing divinity to all existence, and applying the practices of *Yama* and *Niyama* in daily life, then *Santosha* is achieved. Contentment and equanimity come in the mind.

A person does not feel inferior or superior. All the mental complexes become settled and the individual gains a rational grasp of him or herself. The fetters of the complexes in the mind become thinned and finally broken altogether. He or she feels self-fulfilled. There is no need to run after wealth or power. The person need not have all of these things to be fulfilled. He is fulfilled in himself.

However, most people are like children who need to feel their mother's love. When the mother is gone, a small child will often cry and feel unsafe in her absence. The little one may wonder how to get food, how to avoid hunger. Who will help? The child may feel deeply frightened, needy and alone. When the mother comes back, then the child feels safe again. Yet later, when the child grows to be a man or a woman, the fearful neediness from the experience remains inside. The person still does not feel safe or secure about having what is needed.

Thus neediness is formed within the mind and heart of a person. Then people try to cover the neediness by grasping for this and for that. When they get what they desire, it is the same as when their mother came into the room, took them in her arms, fed them and held them. They feel completely safe with the acquisition, at least temporarily. They have grown to be in big bodies and are not looking for the mother but, nonetheless, their minds are still childlike, needy and unfulfilled.

Oftentimes, people will grow in the body but in the mind, their childhood needs remain. Such a needy mind is in pain. To maintain contentment, all of these basic needs must be addressed. They cannot be denied. However, many people have learned to seek the fulfillment of these basic needs in the wrong way. They think if the bank account is high, the house is large and the children are there, they will be safe and happy. Yet, these approaches fail to secure lasting happiness.

Finding Peace

When a person wants to feel like a babe in the mother's arms, he must find his true Mother; he must find the Divine. He has sought in the finite world to satiate his needs but the world cannot satisfy the needs of a human being. Only the Divine can give lasting fulfillment. Contemplation of the infinite and the attribution of divine consciousness to all life bring the experience of peace of mind and contentment. Then the superiority and inferiority complexes of the mind dissolve.

This serenity develops by concentration upon the Divine. When the mind surges in worldly desires, then all equanimity and peace are lost. The mind is rushing here and there. When this happens, it is pulled into the tumultuous waves of this manifest universe and is bouncing up and down. This is the mind's normal state when the practices of *Yama* and *Niyama* are not done.

To develop serenity and equanimity requires not only action but knowledge as well. One must acquire knowledge of the Infinite. There are three ways to acquire this divine knowledge. One is through selfless action. Another is through study, developing understanding and insight into the qualities and characteristics of the infinite Being. The third is to enter into the sacred experience of direct knowing through union with that Divine. Through these practices, knowledge, purity of mind and contentment become available.

This is the path of equanimity. Remember that even in the harshest circumstances it is but the play of *Prakriti* (nature). Remember that you, oh human being, are far more and far deeper than the ups and downs of your daily existence. For in you is the river of conscious awareness, the flow of the Eternal. Dive deep into this subterranean stream and all the dust and dirt of your outer existence will be washed clean and you will find contentment. Do not shirk your responsibilities, run away to a distant mountain or hide from the world. This will not lead you to your goal. Learn instead to stay ever yourself, content within your own being, despite any circumstance, criticism, conflicts or difficulties.

YOU MAY WORK TOWARD WORLD PEACE BUT YOU MUST ALSO WORK ON DEVELOPING INNER PEACE.

Once you have this inner equanimity then you may become a peacemaker. If you would have a world in which peace reigns, develop inner peace and reflect it outwardly. World peace is attained by living beings when the society becomes sufficiently developed to allow for the differences of its members without becoming oppressive toward those who are of a different bent. When tolerance is practiced and inner peace cultivated, then and only then will you make progress. So you may work toward world peace but you must also work on developing inner peace. Then surely you will have success.

Tapas
Discipline and Selfless Love

Tapas means heat or fire. It involves burning away our small sense of self in the fire of selfless love in order to be able to know the nature of the divine Self. *Tapas* is often referred to as self-discipline or austerity that involves practices to curb self-centered and self-indulgent tendencies that build identity with the ego. In the true practice of *Tapas*, energy is focused not by harsh self-punishing disciplines and austerities but by the practice of love. This practice teaches you how to sacrifice self-centered thoughts and actions in the fire of selflessness. It burns the ego on the sacrificial fires of this selfless love. Austerity comes not in mortifying the body but in learning truly to love selflessly, as God loves. This is the discipline of *Tapas*.

In the practice of *Tapas* one performs actions that aid living beings without thought of what will be received in return. In fact, acts of *Tapas* often entail some form of self-sacrifice or selflessness, however small or simple. Service is rendered to others without seeking anything in return. You merely seek to improve the life of another, to aid the welfare of society, to give to others what is their due and what is their need. You act so that they may have a better life, so that they may be happy, so that they may know infinite love. To feed the poor, to give shelter to the homeless, to do a kind act to an older person needing a hand, to remember a child

SACRIFICE YOUR SELF-CENTERED THOUGHTS AND ACTIONS IN THE FIRE OF SELFLESSNESS.

and take a little time to read with her, these are all *Tapas*. Many acts of *seva* (service), are forms of *Tapas*, particularly when you do them with a pure and selfless attitude wanting nothing in return.

As in all of the practices of *Yama* and *Niyama*, intent is key. If the intent is not pure, the mental result will not be the same. *Tapas* begins with the intention to give your time and service to those who are less fortunate than yourself or have some special need. It entails giving that service without desiring something in return, without any secret motives. When practicing *Tapas*, you give selflessly and something happens over time. A purity of mind and heart develops. A contentment arises and a feeling of compassion, of infinite love for all beings. *Tapas* is the tool to develop this compassion and also the expression of this compassion.

It is the approach you take, the motivation you have and the care you take for others that makes *Tapas* work. When done with right motivation, your actions are not for your own benefit, not to achieve your own ends or gain favor with people. When you begin to pride yourself on being selfless, on giving things to people, feeding or sheltering people and want to build your reputation through these actions, then your actions, no matter how helpful, are not *Tapas*. This is because, in reality, you are using the people to achieve a personal end.

Instead, give to them because you love them. Give to them because they are in need. Give to them and expect nothing. If they forget about you, then they forget about you. If they applaud you and sing your praises, what of it? You do these actions out of pure love. Then, over time, it is not just this project or that act that is *Tapas*. The psychology of selfless love becomes a mental attitude toward all beings, toward all life.

Self-Sacrifice

With *Tapas*, selfless service for others is done without thought of reward, and often *Tapas* involves some form of personal sacrifice. However, it has mistakenly been taken by some to mean to harm yourself in some way, to beat yourself, starve your body, think of yourself as a lowly being, worse than anyone else, wearing rags and being impoverished. This has often been considered a form of pious self-sacrifice and thus *Tapas*. Some *yogis*, as well as monks, would beat themselves to practice self-sacrifice. They thought that if they inflicted pain upon their person, they would somehow be purified and all ill thoughts and actions atoned for. However, self-harm does not lead to a pure heart and clear mind. To mutilate the temple of God, the body that has been given to you, is not *Tapas*. It has nothing to do with *Tapas*.

DISSOLVE THE SEEDS OF SELFISHNESS IN THE OCEAN OF UNCONDITIONAL LOVE.

A pure heart and a clear mind are developed by dissolving the seeds of selfishness in the ocean of unconditional love. The discipline of *Tapas* is one of curbing self-absorption and self-centeredness not of punishing yourself. Never think you are inferior or less than anyone, nor that you are superior to anyone. You are a child of the Divine. You do not need prideful self-defense. Nor do you need to diminish what you are or what you have done to love selflessly.

With *Tapas,* you sacrifice through unconditional love and selfless service to others. Even practiced in the smallest way, such as a kind word that you didn't need to say, a thoughtful act, washing a dish for someone, letting another go ahead of you in line, even simple random acts of kindness can be *Tapas* when done with an attitude of selflessness and love. The key is selfless, self-sacrificing love, to serve another with a pure heart and no intention whatsoever of personal gain.

The true sacrifice given in *Tapas* is to let go of absorption in your personal sense of ego and the distortions of reality that arise out of this ego identity. You sacrifice your identity on the altar of truth in deep unconditional love, your sense of *I and mine,* your belief that you are separate from others, your obsession with taking care of number one first. The result is the ability to know the real from the unreal, to **THERE IS NO ROOM IN SPIRITUAL LIFE FOR SELF-CENTEREDNESS.** see all beings as part of an integrated whole and to dissolve your individual ego into awareness of a unified, transcendent, conscious existence. Know that you are so much more than a tiny person in a body. You are a part of the vast whole of being, of one love, of one heart, one indivisible divine Self.

The Practice

To practice *Tapas* in your life as you go through your day, just think each moment, "Is there someone I can help even in the smallest way this very moment?" You will be surprised how much you can do for others. In quiet ways, in small ways you may express pure and selfless love – just a little touch, a kind word, a small help with some difficulty.

Tapas is not necessarily an action that you plan for, such as a service project you do on the weekend. This is a good way to start but over time this selfless service needs to continue for twenty-four hours every day and not just four hours once a week or simply four hours each day. Become immersed in the attitude of *Tapas*, so that every word that comes from your lips, every move of your hand is an action of selfless love.

There is no room in spiritual life for self-centeredness. When the mental tendency arises to overly identify with *I, me and mine*, counterbalance it with actions that expand your awareness of others. Selfless love and service help you connect with life and see beyond yourself. Without this selfless love and service, the worms of selfishness eat into you. Service to living beings is an integral part of yoga and meditation because love unconditional is at the heart of all spiritual practice.

Your Intentions

Many actions may appear to be service but, in fact, are not service because the motivation is incorrect. Acts of service require more than merely performing the action, for actions may be done for many reasons. If an action is done with the intention to promote personal benefit and the ego, that action is not a service to anyone regardless of how it may appear. Actions that may, to the casual observer, appear not to serve anyone may be great acts of service. Service is not defined by a specific act but by the intention with which the action is performed.

Even handing a glass of water to another with pure

intentions and kindness may be an act of great service. Even such simple actions can be selfless. Another act, even as important as starting a children's home or a home for the aged, may not be *Tapas* if done to make a good impression, make money or acquire name and fame. The apparent social act of goodness may become an act of exploitation. Those who are in the homes may suffer because the person operating the home has selfish motivations. The operator may cut costs on supplying food to make a little extra money or do similar acts of greed and unkindness. It happens like this.

THE SPIRIT OF TAPAS COMES EVEN IN THE WORKPLACE.

When the selfless love of *Tapas* serves those in need, the motivation of greed cannot remain. You may earn money by serving others, but if money is your sole motivation, the service is lost. When immersed in giving to others, selfless love needs to be present. If you act solely for the purpose of getting something for yourself, then you have lost *Tapas*. There is no *Tapas*. Even if you are working in a service-oriented job but your intention is to make your quota, to get through the work with as little effort as possible and get paid, you may do acts that hopefully help people, but the service opportunity is lost. However, if in this same environment, you focus on the needs of the people you are working with and how you can help them rather than your own needs and you go the extra mile for them, then the spirit of *Tapas* comes even in the workplace. Just because it is a job does not mean you cannot practice *Tapas*. Just because you have a family life does not mean you cannot practice *Tapas*.

By doing *Tapas*, thinking of the welfare of others and caring for their needs, you move beyond the limited sense of *I and mine* to see a world of vital living beings and their suffering. A little compassionate love goes a long way in this world. When kind-hearted love is present, purity of mind also comes and finally contentment. All of the mental distortions, the seeking and the needing become calmed.

Yama and *Niyama* embrace fundamental approaches to daily life that all who follow the spiritual path need to incorporate in one form or another to be able to walk the path. It does not matter whether you are Hindu, Christian, Jewish, Buddhist, Sufi or Muslim. It does not matter what you call these practices. They are necessary because the monkey mind will wander here and there. When it is not given direction, it will never be able to settle down and gain the capacity to reflect on its infinite essence. The different tenets of *Yama* and *Niyama* combine as one practice. They are a practical life-supporting, deeply connected way of being in the world that teaches us to live in love.

Svadhyaya
Reflection Upon the Nature of the Soul

"Great lions can find peace in a cage.
But we should only do that as a last resort.
So those bars I see that restrain your wings,
I guess you won't mind if I pry them open."
RUMI

Svadhyaya is the search for knowledge and the practice of understanding truth. The word comes from the root *sva* (soul or self) and *dhyaya*, rooted in the word *dhyia* (to meditate, reflect upon, study or contemplate). Thus, *Svadhyaya* connotes self-study or reflection upon the nature of the soul or *Atman*.

When practicing the self-study of *Svadhyaya*, you seek to comprehend the nature of your own consciousness. You explore the nature of your own existence and the nature of this manifest universe. Thus you gain knowledge of the underlying consciousness that is quiescent in all of existence. To do this, there are both external and internal practices.

The External Practice

Svadhyaya involves acquainting yourself with the true knowledge that underlies all existence. The external practice may involve reading inspiring books, blogs and articles or going to lectures, seminars or trainings that help you better understand yourself and your deeper nature. You may read holy scriptures that inspire the mind toward the Divine. You may

SELF-STUDY BEGINS WITH STUDYING THE KNOWLEDGE REALIZED AND RECORDED BY OTHERS

listen to the ideas of others, attending lectures and workshops that help you to understand yourself. You may read scientific material that inspires you. Or you may go to teachers or gurus to learn from their words of wisdom and their personal experiences. All of this research and inquiry helps you to gain information and experiences that may inspire the mind and assist you to know the nature of your own existence. These are the basic external practices of *Svadhyaya*.

Inquiring from sources around you that can inform you about reality and build your personal knowledge base is the first step in getting to know yourself. It gives you the benefit of the experience of others. Reading books or scriptures such as the *Bhagavad Gita*, the *Upanishads*, the *Yoga Sutras* or other spiritual texts can help a great deal in clarifying confusions in your mind and will introduce concepts that you may not have been aware of. It can expand your mind, leaving you better prepared intellectually to contemplate your own nature. This practice is emphasized in *Jnani Yoga*, the yoga of knowledge. When your mind is confused about the nature of reality and ignorant of truth, it is very hard to know the Self. Self-study begins with studying the knowledge realized and recorded by others and thus expanding your own knowledge base.

POETRY THAT SPEAKS THE LANGUAGE OF THE HEART HOLDS TRUTHS ONLY THE HEART CAN RECOGNIZE.

However, knowledge is not only for the mind. It is also for the heart. Learning about devotion, singing the names of the gods and goddesses, chanting, doing *kirtan*, listening to stories of the lives and experiences of spiritual women and men open the heart. This is another form in which knowledge can come to you. Even myths and stories bring spiritual inspiration and hold the wisdom of the ages. Also, poetry that speaks the language of the heart holds truths only the heart can recognize; it gives wisdom and opens a doorway. The heart knows truth, recognizes it. Let these sources of divine knowledge and wisdom awaken your heart and inspire you to Self-knowledge.

Also there is great benefit from being in the presence of spiritual masters and holy men and women. Many radiate a presence that has a direct influence on your mind, bringing it to a more subtle awareness. When this happens, you are able to perceive subtle reality directly. Spiritual realizations open within you due to contact with elevated beings. It is one of the best ways to begin to experience Divine Consciousness. Of course, as you progress in your development, it is important to be able to access these states of awareness and wisdom on your own. Still a little grace of an awakened one or even the presence of a man or woman of wisdom can be very beneficial.

Part of spiritual life is keeping the company of others who are seekers on the spiritual path. This *satsanga* or *samgha* (spiritual community) assists you to stay focused on spiritual life and not become confused by day-to-day distractions, the ideas and beliefs of those caught entirely in the quagmire of everyday life. For those who have eyes to see and ears to hear, even the bird singing in the tree, the babbling brook or the sunrise can teach you knowledge of the Self within. Life is an interwoven network from the smallest grain of sand to the vast ocean, a wholeness of being that can teach you the secrets of the eternal Self. In the practice of *Svadhyaya*, being a humble student willing to learn from all creation allows you to access true Self-knowledge.

You may read holy books and study external sources of wisdom to enhance your knowledge of the essential nature of reality. It may be that you will read books, go to talks and so on but *Svadhyaya* is not based on external learning alone. The knowledge you learn from others may be a fundamental starting point to true knowledge but it is not the knowledge itself. It is only the finger that points the way so that the mind knows to move in that direction and continue until the shores of Self-knowledge are reached.

The Internal Practice

The internal practice of *Svadhyaya* is deeply contemplative. It involves truthful (*Satya*) self-observation and self-reflection. This may take the form of impartially observing your thoughts, words and behaviors or sitting in silent meditation and studying the Self within. This internal practice of *Svadhyaya* awakens when you take the knowledge that you acquire through your study and research and integrate it into your own experience.

Whether it be through your self-observation, self-study, contemplation or meditation, you begin to access knowledge of the Self. When the knowledge you have learned awakens your own essential being, you come in contact with the infinite source of knowledge within you. For, in fact, all knowledge lies within.

At this stage, you may attain direct access to the infinite knowledge that lies within the minds of all beings. You develop your intuition and you become able to access intuitional knowledge. When this happens, you will automatically know what is real and what is illusion. You will know when someone is exploitive and when he is not. You will understand clearly what is a selfless act and what is not a selfless act. You will have no problem in perceiving the dirt in the mind and how you can wash it away. You will have no problem in understanding that you are not inferior or superior to anyone. You will have no problem to perceive directly every molecule, every atom of this expressed world as a manifestation of divinity. You will have no problem to perceive the love that is the underlying essence of existence.

Developing Spiritual Discrimination

When a person doing meditation reaches a certain stage in the practice, an understanding arises of the difference between those forces that propel a human being toward divinity and those forces that degenerate the consciousness of a living being. This ability to discriminate between these two opposing forces is called *viveka* in Sanskrit. This is true discrimination, which distinguishes between the real and the unreal. This Self-knowledge comes from the supra-psychic stratum of the mind.

True discrimination is a very subtle ability that awakens not by intellectual effort but by sincere and piercing meditation that leads the meditator to deeper Self-knowledge. When this spiritual knowledge awakens, *buddhi* (intuitional wisdom) pierces the veil of illusion and you may grasp truth. To practice truly all of the aspects of *Yama* and *Niyama*, you need some degree of discrimination. Discrimination is based in knowledge. Without discrimination, how are you to tell what is going toward the One and what is pulling away? To be able to determine this, you must have discrimination that comes when the mind is made pure through the practice of *Yama* and *Niyama*.

One might think that a sharp intellect is needed for spiritual discrimination but the way of the intellect is a crooked road. It is the longest path to *viveka* (knowing the real from the unreal). Real discrimination does not come from the mere study of books. A person may be very sharp-witted and very clever, but this does not mean he or she possesses true discrimination. Exercise of the intellectual mind means nothing in the face of true knowledge. The knowledge acquired through worldly experience is one sort. The knowledge acquired through inner research is another. These two bodies of knowledge cannot be compared as they are altogether different.

PUT ASIDE ALL INTELLECTUAL ARROGANCE AND SURRENDER YOURSELF HUMBLY BEFORE YOUR DIVINE SOURCE.

Yet there is one commonality between them. They both require engagement of the mind. In one, the mind pursues the colors of this world and in the other, the intellect searches the inner realms, piercing the outer layers of the mind to reach a state of pinnacled intellect in which the mind becomes clear and calm, devoid of all blemishes. In this state alone *viveka* or discrimination is clearly established.

Such a pinnacled intellect devoid of habitual mental tendencies *(samskaras)* may see beyond the veil of illusionary experience into the very core of the Cosmic Mind. The soul is revealed. Such an intellect becomes the witness of the fascinating qualities and characteristics of the infinite *Brahma*. Such an intellect will grasp the subtle sweetness of the Infinite. Such an intellect will know the difference between what is real and what is illusion.

If you want this discriminative knowledge, do not engage in idle or useless talk and do not use your mind for endless debate. Put aside all intellectual arrogance and surrender yourself humbly before your divine Source. Arrogance of knowledge, culture and vanity of good deeds are impediments to the development of discrimination. Humility, kind acts, self-surrender and love will enhance the capacity for discrimination and thus the Self-knowledge of *Svadhyaya*.

The Intellect, Courage and Equilibrium

It is important to develop a base for intellectual growth in spiritual life. If intellectual growth is just reading books, argument and debate, it is virtually useless. It may be good for the study of a particular academic interest but the intellect is a very deceptive mechanism. A human being can have many beliefs without realizing that those ideas are motivated by social politeness, a need for acceptance or some other emotional need.

Unless there is self-reflection and an effort to develop the mind in spiritual contemplation, the intellect only becomes self-rationalizing and can, in fact, be a source of deception and delusion. If you wish to move beyond this, you must be courageous, willing to examine and face hidden motives, unconsciousness and self-deception.

Intellectual courage is important in psycho-spiritual development. When you do not have the courage to develop a pinnacled, discriminating intellect, then you will find that the capacity to know truth will evade you. The development of a one-pointed intellect can only come when you develop courage in the intellectual realm to bring the mind away from all of its normal trappings into a kind of concentrated trance in which there is the development of discrimination. When a human being has courage, he or she may move beyond social norms and outward-oriented behavior to pierce the veil of self-deceit and social conformity.

Such a one may look within, using rationality and intuition, focusing the intellect so that the barriers to truth are broken and the mind becomes capable of staying in a state of equilibrium. With equilibrium comes the capacity to focus and concentrate the intellect still more, to bring it to a single point that can then delve into the mysteries beyond intellect.

Self-Reflection, Love and Contemplation

If you have a fine intellect, a brilliant mind, let it be offered to the Divine. Let that brilliance be a gift to your deepest Self. Do not waste it. Bring it to that inner guide. Surrender it before your divine Source so that it may open your heart because knowledge of the mind devoid of love is nothing short of delusion.

The knowledge of a mind imbued with love will benefit all. Use your intellect, not to bring darkness and argument to you but to pierce the veil of self-deceit and become aware of divine qualities. Then you will have a knowledge that cannot be lost, that is permanent. Know that eternal Self

IF YOU HAVE A FINE INTELLECT, A BRILLIANT MIND, LET IT BE OFFERED TO THE DIVINE.

and you will know all. Use your discrimination to distinguish between what is of the Divine and what pulls you away from the Divine.

When you practice self-reflecting contemplation then the nature of consciousness will begin to dawn in your mind. The qualities and characteristics of the infinite Being will become perceptible to you. You will begin to understand the meaning of justice. Truth will be a word you know and understand. Love, compassion, and beauty all will become fully comprehensible to you and knowledge of the Infinite will dawn in the mind. This is the practice of *Svadhyaya*.

Ishvara Pranidhana
Surrender to God

"There is a divine world of light with many suns in the sky.
I slept with my Lord one night,
now all that is luminous I know we conceived."
St. Teresa of Avila

Ishvara Pranidhana is a practice of self-surrender in deep contemplation of the eternal source of all. *Ishvara* connotes God, *Brahma*, Lord of this universe.

Historically, people have given it slightly different meanings but they all point to a higher power, a consciousness greater than our individual sense of self. *Pranidhana* also has multiple connotations but primarily means fixing attention on the Divine through meditation or prayer and generally implies self-surrender.

IF YOU ARE TO KNOW INFINITE CONSCIOUSNESS, YOU MUST COME IN DIRECT CONTACT WITH THAT CONSCIOUSNESS.

This practice is one of surrendering your ideas, beliefs, constructs, control and most importantly your sense of self to the one Self, to pure essential being, to the Lord, God, the infinite *Brahma,* however you express it for yourself, your Source. Inherent in this practice is knowledge of something greater than your small ego existence. If you let go and surrender, you just might get over yourself enough to perceive the immense shower of grace flowing from the eternal Divinity. And if you really let go, you just might melt into that ocean of love. It is through surrendering to this infinite Self in the practice of *Ishvara Pranidhana* that the deep Self-knowledge of *Svadhyaya* arises and that all of the practices of *Yama* and *Niyama* really come into focus. Without *Ishvara Pranidhana,* it is not possible really to do the other practices. *Ishvara Pranidhana* is the base of all practices of *Yama* and *Niyama.* If you are to know Divine Consciousness, you must come in direct contact with that consciousness. With direct contact, harmlessness, truth, integrity, purity of heart and mind, equanimity, and Self-knowledge become more accessible.

Divine connection and the cultivation of the wisdom of *Yama* and *Niyama* go hand-in-hand. When you do the practices of *Yama* and *Niyama,* you purify the mind. At the same time when you ideate upon the Infinite in meditation, there is direction and focus for the mind. Without focus, your efforts become scattered and unproductive. Through meditation and self-surrender in *Ishvara Pranidhana,* you come in direct contact with divine Presence.

Ishvara Pranidhana allows you to focus all of your concentration upon the controlling point of this entire universe, often called *Ishvara.* This sublime Cosmic Consciousness, manifesting as the nexus of the entire manifest universe, is the Soul of your soul, the heart of your heart. When in your meditation you focus your mind in full surrender to the divine God Self, the nucleus of existence, then, by grace, it may become known.

The practice of *Ishvara Pranidhana* focuses upon this cosmic Self. When you first begin meditative practice, you may find you are spending all your time trying to concentrate. However, as you begin the practices of *Yama* and *Niyama*, you will find that your concentration in meditation grows better and better. *SURRENDER YOUR NORMAL RESTLESSNESS OF MIND, BELIEFS AND NEED FOR CONTROL.* When your lifestyle is made subtle with these practices, concentration is enhanced.

As concentration is enhanced, a deeper knowledge of the Infinite arises. The noises about you when you meditate cease to bother you. The internal chatter of the mind, like the noise around you, does not bother you because you are focusing on something much more profound. As you focus your awareness on the profound consciousness that underlies all manifestation, you find that you begin to have a resonance with that infinite Divine Consciousness.

The Mind

There are certain basic qualities that everyone's mind possesses. The first is that mind is not static; it is in a perpetual process of movement. The second basic characteristic of mind is that it is malleable; whatever it moves toward, it takes the likeness of. Whatever you focus on, you tend to become absorbed in. When you frequently think of a material object and have a strong desire for it, then it will fill your awareness. As you continue to focus on the object of interest, the mind becomes more and more absorbed in the object until the image of it is fixed in the mind and your thoughts and feelings begin to revolve around it.

In the practice of *Ishvara Pranidhana*, the characteristic movement and malleability of the mind is utilized to gain vision of the Infinite. The infinite cosmic Source, the controlling point of the entire manifest universe and of the unmanifest universe becomes the focus of your attention. When ideation upon infinite consciousness becomes your focus, then the first characteristic of the mind, mental movement, is set in motion toward the divine Self.

As you continue to concentrate your attention in meditation upon the Divine, the second characteristic of mind, malleability, comes into play and the mind begins to take on the qualities and characteristics of that infinite Self. *NONE OF THIS IS POSSIBLE* You become absorbed in the *WHEN WE STAY WITHIN THE* experience. This absorption in *CONFINES OF OUR MENTAL* your divine focus of attention *CONSTRUCTS AND BELIEFS.* is called *samadhi.* In this state, you become one with that upon which you have been concentrating. You surrender your normal restlessness of mind, beliefs and need for control to that which is far greater than your personal ego self.

The Sadhana Process: The Practices

The process of surrender in meditation on the Divine is the fundamental practice of *Ishvara Pranidhana.* The process entails contemplation, prayer, silent meditation on the one eternal essence of all with an attitude of complete humility and surrender of your beliefs, constructs and control.

Letting go of your thoughts, beliefs and ideas and surrender to the Divine is *sadhana*, meditative practice. Real meditation cannot be done without self-surrender. Otherwise we are just wandering around within the confines of the ego and the thoughts in the mind. It is only when we are ready to let go, to trust and to entrust our welfare to something more, something greater than our individuality that the numinous opens to us. When we simply let go of striving, achieving, trying to figure it out and somehow fix it, when we simply offer it and open up, then the shower of grace can be felt. Then the light of that beyond thoughts or beliefs pierces the veil of our ignorance and truth is revealed.

None of this is possible when we stay within the confines of our mental constructs and beliefs. To know the vast ocean of Divinity that is our source and our home, it is necessary to let go, surrender, quiet the monkey mind and sink beneath the surface waves of our existence. The practice of *Ishvara Pranidhana* gives us opportunity for knowing the depths in our meditation, in our contemplations and in our prayers.

If you are inclined to prayer, do not pray to get this or that. The Divine knows what you need. Pray instead affirming your surrender to God. "Not my will but Thy will." If you are inclined to *puja* (ritual offerings to God), this also can be a beneficial practice of *Ishvara Pranidhana*, but only when done truly from the heart and not for show or just because everyone else is doing it or expects it of you. If you do puja sincerely offering all that you have and all that you are to the lotus feet of your chosen Deity, if you let go of beliefs and thoughts and suspend your mind in devotion, surely the heart will open, the mind will quiet and one true divine Self will appear.

Singing the names of God, telling stories of saints, sages and divine beings, doing *kirtan* (chanting God's name) or engaging in any of the ways people find connection to the Divine are all practices of *Ishvara Pranidhana*, are ways to surrender to the Divine. Of all of these practices of *Ishvara Pranidhana*, surely the deepest is silent meditation. In meditation, all thoughts are surrendered and in the stillness of being, the heart and mind open to the ocean of Divinity.

DIVINITY IS IN EVERY EXPRESSION OF THIS UNIVERSE

Without the support of all of the *Yama* and *Niyama* practices, this opening in *Ishvara Pranidhana* is not possible because the light of the infinite Divinity cannot dawn in a mind that is cluttered and discontent. When there is truth, harmony, contentment, purity, selfless love and knowledge of the nature of reality, then meditation upon the Divine can bring you to the shores of eternity and realization of the Self.

The call of your meditation is to perceive Divinity. When you let go and surrender to your Higher Power, you can come to know the pure undifferentiated essence that lies within. Divinity is in every expression of this universe. When you respect it, appreciate it, treat all beings with kindness, it comes closer to you. Your vision expands. When you utilize your discrimination to maintain this perception, again your vision expands.

The Meditation Experience: The Inner Sanctuary

The inner sanctuary is that indwelling heart-cave found in the depths of your meditation, in your *Brahma sadhana*. This is where you truly surrender to God, where the heart opens fully and you let go, dissolving in the arms of love. Meditation is the core practice of *Ishvara Pranidhana* and thus central to *Yama* and *Niyama*. Understanding meditation practice and how to work with the process that happens as you sink deeper and deeper toward inner union is important in *Ishvara Pranidhana* and thus requires some explanation.

Many barriers may arise to finding that indwelling heart-cave where the stillness, the peace, the bliss, love and union abide. Barriers come in the *MANY BARRIERS MAY ARISE TO FINDING THAT INDWELLING HEART-CAVE.* mind and in the body, in the aches and pains and problems of the body, in hearing sounds around you, the phone ringing, traffic noises, in feeling sleepy, in mental thoughts that preoccupy the mind with worries, concerns, responsibilities and so on.

Even finding the discipline simply to sit for meditation can be difficult. The minute you sit, you may begin to think about all the things you need to do or someone you are having difficulty with. Endless creative thought-streams may fill your mind. You have forgotten them all day but the moment you sit quietly, they pop in; isn't it true? Then the overriding desire of all the muscles in your body is to jump up and run around doing, doing, doing.

When this happens, take a few deep breaths and start your practice again. If you must, write yourself a note so you won't forget it later and then say, "All right, I put it in the note. Now it is out of my mind." The monkey mind becomes a problem when it wants to go here and there and everywhere, to wander around in all of its troubles and concerns and worries about this and that. Your mantra (sacred sound for meditation) is like a lodestone to bring you back in harmony with the breath, to here and now, to the moment. Finally, if you keep returning to your mantra, eventually the mind gets tired of running about and starts to concentrate on the focus of meditation practice.

During meditation, in *dharana*, the phase of concentration, the mind struggles to get a little bit of focus. At first, so many waves are in the mind. Your mind engages with thoughts, with the senses, with the physical body and then with the memories. Engagement with the body, the senses, your thoughts, memories and feelings in the lower layers (*koshas*) of the mind absorbs your attention during this phase of concentration. Then a flow begins to occur in the waves of the mind and you enter into *dhyana*, into actual meditation. In this phase of your practice, the mind begins to be in harmony with its object of ideation. Then through mantra or other practices, you keep returning to the sound, the breath, the meaning. You keep returning to your *dhyana*, your flow toward the Divine, and then slowly, slowly, all these sensory engagements, memories, concerns, worries, issues in relationship to your senses and your life in the world begin to lessen. Your mind spends more and more time in concentrated focus.

Your mind cannot grasp the infinite, formless and timeless *Brahma* as an object of your meditation; for this concept is beyond the comprehension of the mind. Whatever your approach, you will find that Cosmic Consciousness as an object of meditation is beyond the scope of mind. It is like a *koan*, a spiritual riddle in the Zen tradition. You are given something to concentrate on that is so large, without directional points, vast, timeless, formless and incomprehensible to the rational mind.

The rational mind wants to put things in sequences. It wants to have a beginning, middle and end. So what is a good focus for your concentration in meditation? Something you simply cannot comprehend. That is the *koan*, the dilemma set by your meditation practice. You are given something to comprehend that your mind simply cannot comprehend.

WHEN THE MIND STARTS TO GIVE UP, IT STOPS MAKING SUCH A RACKET.

So you keep trying, thinking about it and trying to find a way to box it in to some kind of sentence structure, some sort of linear approach but your mind keeps falling short. At first, the mind cannot even focus upon your object of ideation. It is too abstract, too difficult. The mind wanders. Then it focuses on distractions, perhaps a loud noise outside or someone talking nearby.

In this way, your mind creates distractions to avoid concentrating on something that it really cannot wrap itself around because it is just too big. It doesn't fit in a linear thought. Then again, you focus back to your breath and the sound of mantra, remember the ideation, then slowly, slowly the mind begins to wear itself out and to harmonize. It begins to give up, surrender, let go. When the mind starts to give up, it stops making such a racket. It just gets tired after a while. You get tired of thinking and then you actually concentrate.

Then something happens. Suddenly, experience happens, moods shifts and feelings change. Subtle waves form in the mind. They do not precisely have form. They are not linear thoughts. In fact, the thinking mind becomes a little quiet. It doesn't have so much to think about. If it begins to think, it tends to think about the object of ideation. It begins to think about the nature of *Brahma* and eventually it stops thinking altogether and starts being, feeling and experiencing directly.

At this stage, you have moved beyond the lower layers or *koshas* of the mind, governed by *manas* (rational mind), into *buddhi*, (intuitive mind) and the causal layers of your mind.

As you continue to deepen your meditation you come in contact with the bliss body. In these subtle layers of your being, the first experience is a direct touch with the realm of creativity. You may notice creative imagery, an intuitive sense of things, intuitive feelings and that you know things. You may notice blissful, expansive feelings as well. Out of this realm has come many of the world's greatest creative expressions and knowledge. The great arts, heavenly music, the great scientific theories all come from this realm.

In deep meditation, as your mind grows in magnitude; you access the next stratum of being, the knowledge body, *Vijnanamaya Kosha,* where all knowledge and wisdom become available. From this stratum, knowledge flows and becomes creativity that moves into the rational mind and begins to express in linear thought. The knowledge comes from a realm that is non-linear, where linear thought does not exist. You experience sweet, blissful knowingness, the wisdom of the ancients, the sense of truth, knowing the real from the unreal and the sense of infinite association. You feel unity with the infinite divine Being. You experience communion and knowledge. A great deal of bliss begins to form in the mind.

As you continue to deepen your meditation you come in contact with the bliss body. In this sphere, divine bliss becomes your body and you feel the exquisite bliss of divine union. You feel that you are one with the infinite Source, that you and your beloved Lord are one. In this *ananda* (bliss body) you experience direct communion in ecstasy. White light may permeate your awareness or you may experience being enveloped in the golden egg of the divine Being. There are no distinctive needs, no thoughts. Time and space become irrelevant, as theories. There is the exquisiteness of being, the fulfillment of one's heart and mind.

In direct communion, the thoughts in the mind are suspended. There is no need for thoughts. Your mind and individual sense of self become completely immersed in the cosmic mind and you feel that only God exists. Only the divine *Brahma* exists. You feel no sense of separation. There is no *I and thou* experience at all. There is only the infinite, cosmic Self, in which the whole universe abides. You may feel, "I am that cosmic Entity." No sense of separation is there. When meditation brings you to this state, there is no sense of individuality, only cosmic existence, sometimes called *Saguna Brahma*.

If, by grace, you should be swept deeper still, you move beyond the manifest universe into the unmanifest or *Nirguna Brahma,* where there is no form, no body, and even the bliss body has dissolved. This is the still center of all that is. If you should access this deepest reality, it is without qualities of any sort. The manifest universe is *saguna,* (with qualities), the unmanifest is *nirguna,* (without qualities); that is, without time, space or causality. This is the pure *Parama Purusha,* pure consciousness. The matrix of creation is quiescent. There is not even bliss or the cosmic *I-am.* All has become quiescent; all seeds are burnt. There is no mind. There is no memory. There is no movement. It is pure, awakened, conscious being outside of time and space.

Should you go to that realm, when you return to the realm of manifestation, you will feel great bliss, will feel a great knowledge. A part of you will remain timeless. This experience, this *samadhi* (state of divine absorption), can be maintained for up to twenty-one days in a physical form. Beyond that time, the physical form cannot be maintained and you stay forever in the timeless realm, leaving your body.

One who touches this realm is entirely free but when the seeds of *samskara* (mental tendencies) remain, the consciousness will be brought again into the manifest realm to play once again in the halls of creation, to be woven again into the tapestry of life, change, and expression by the creative principle of nature.

Madhuvidya: Meditation in the World
In addition to the practice of surrendering everything in meditation upon the Great, there is a practice of *Ishvara*

Pranidhana that can be done while involved in your daily activities. It is said that to one who can see, this ordinary world becomes sublime. If, while living and acting in the world we focus on the divine nature of what is around us, we turn the ordinary into something extraordinary. When we see the infinite *Brahma* in every object, every person we meet, every action we do, when we immerse our minds in this vision of the sublime,

TO ONE WHO CAN SEE, THIS ORDINARY WORLD BECOMES SUBLIME.

then we surrender our false beliefs unto the lotus feet of immortal truth. We learn to be in the world but not of it. We see God everywhere. We see ourselves in all beings and all beings as part of our Self. This surrender of our false sense of self and perceptions based in ego identity is *madhu vidya,* sweet knowledge.

When we dedicate all our desires, all our actions to the Divine, the constrictions that bind us begin to soften. If you desire something, remember what you really want. The mind seeks divinity in all its desires and the heart in its longing to love and to be loved. Remember, it is that one Beloved you are searching for in all that you desire and remember that all that you have in your life are gifts to you. The divine One is always caring for you, coming in so many ways and forms to take care of you for you are a child of the Divine and that One will always care for you.

When you practice this remembrance that all is *Brahma* throughout your day it will help you in your meditation. Keeping the mind pure, the body clean, the thoughts pure and the heart pure will also make the mind fertile for meditation practices. Remembrance of the divine Self in all that you do, giving service to every living being that you encounter without thought of return bring you to a state of simplicity and surrender. Taking an attitude of service in all that you do, even if it is the simplest of tasks awakens awareness. Both in large and small ways you may bring love and beauty to this world when your heart is open and you practice *madhu vidya*, seeing all as Divine.

This practice not only makes the mind fit for meditation but also makes it contented. This feeling of contentment brings you into the realm of spiritual life. Equanimity arises in the mind and a kindness that allows for meditation. The restless and hungry desires begin to subside and you become calm and content, not seeking to be other than what you are. Be who you are, what you are, here and now, and love yourself for your own divine expression. In this contentment there is peace. Release yourself from having to be more, to have more, to impress others, to acquire, to seek. All these things are very wearing. Contentment on the other hand is a very fine experience.

BE WHO YOU ARE, WHAT YOU ARE, HERE AND NOW AND LOVE YOURSELF FOR YOUR OWN DIVINE EXPRESSION.

All the *Yama* and *Niyama* practices help you to enjoy the sweet and infinite ways that divine love is ever showering upon you. With this, you may perceive divinity all around you, closer than you can imagine. This is the great reward for your efforts to practice *Yama* and *Niyama* and the result when you take these practices seriously.

The Experience

When you do the practices of *Ishvara Pranidhana*, you may begin to experience yourself as the One who is in all beings, in all things. You may begin to experience your existence as endless, never having a beginning and never having an end. You are pure and you are formless, without any flaws. When mind dissolves in the whole of being, then you are Infinite Consciousness, the well of love from which this entire universe has sprung. You live in the form of every being. You live in every atom of this manifest universe. You live in the pure essence of self-awareness.

WHEN MIND DISSOLVES IN THE WHOLE OF BEING, THEN YOU ARE INFINITE CONSCIOUSNESS, THE WELL OF LOVE FROM WHICH THIS ENTIRE UNIVERSE HAS SPRUNG.

Over time, the mind, with intense focus upon the Infinite, begins to acquire an identity with infinite Being and a fundamental change occurs. The very qualities and characteristics of the mind become altered in due time so that slowly, slowly the individual loses the sense of separateness. The experience of *the little I* gets absorbed in the experience of the *Cosmic I*, the sense of pure existence in the universe. The conscious awareness of the little person caught in the ego mind gets free and is absorbed in cosmic existence, in the infinite *Purusha*, the unmanifest consciousness that underlies all existence.

The little consciousness that was caught like a drop of water in a glass gets set free, gets dropped again in the ocean of Divine Consciousness. Its essence having always been identical to the infinite Ocean, it cannot be seen as separate from the Ocean. It becomes completely one with that Ocean.

With surrender to the one eternal Self through *Ishvara Pranidhana,* lasting happiness, permanent happiness may be achieved and all of the fetters and bonds of the suffering-mind may be broken. The feeling and experience of separate existence will be lost, and like the babe forever merged in the loving arms of the mother, all desires fulfilled, you will merge in the one true Self from which you have come.

CHAPTER IV

Living Yoga

*"How did the rose ever open its heart
and give to this world all of its beauty?
It felt the encouragement of light against its being,
otherwise we all remain too frightened."*
HAFIZ

Love, Forgiveness, Gratitude and Compassion

*L*ove is a many-faceted topic. There is love between people, love for nature, love for animals and plants and love for the Divine. What is important in all of these different experiences of love is that you love purely. To know infinite love, you need not live up to anyone's expectations, but only take the time to turn your mind and heart toward the Divine and think of the qualities and characteristics of that divine Beloved.

By taking the time to suspend your mind and dissolve your selfhood into that eternal Self of yourself, you will discover the love of which all human love is only a dim reflection. One of the primary characteristics of cosmic love is abundant compassion for all living beings. That cosmic Self loves everyone and everything and sees everyone and everything as a part of its own Self. That Self has infinite love for living beings, infinite love for you. When you emulate this infinite love, this compassionate attitude of cosmic love in your own approach to life, you gain proximity to the Divine.

True love, the deepest form of love, the unconditional love, does not define and is not confined. Experiencing this love, you have care for all beings, including your own self, for you too are the child of the Divine. You are the son or the daughter of the divine One. If anyone should want to harm you, diminish you, hurt you, or tell you that you are less than others, do not listen to them. For all are the children of the Divine, including you, and all are important to that beloved Divinity.

ONE OF THE PRIMARY CHARACTERISTICS OF COSMIC LOVE IS ABUNDANT COMPASSION FOR ALL LIVING BEINGS.

The love of the one Beloved, who is the source of all love, is a shower of grace that falls eternally on all living beings. This love rejects no one. All are precious to that divine Beloved. You cannot earn the love of the Divine. It is not for sale. Instead it is freely given to all who take the time to notice it. To the Divine, those who are praised and those who go unnoticed by others, those who are capable of great deeds and those who give in small ways are all the same. All are parts of one interwoven, interconnected whole. There is not more love for one and less for the other.

If you want to know the Infinite, love for all is the best approach. Even for those who do you harm, love and compassion given freely is the best approach. It doesn't mean you must sanctify their actions or that you need to tolerate hurtful actions. Only ignite the kindness, compassion and caring in your own heart. If you care for others and spend your time in acts of kindness to others, even though you yourself may carry a deep burden of pain, your pain will become less. You will see that in loving and caring for others resides the real reward in this life.

If you want to know the Divinity that is the source of all love, do good deeds throughout your day and throughout your life. Make a point, each and every day, to intentionally do at least one act of kindness for another. This way you develop a kind heart. Developing a kind *IF YOU WANT TO KNOW THE INFINITE, LOVE FOR ALL IS THE BEST APPROACH.* heart is the key step to the development of great compassion. To know great compassion is to know love unconditional. To know love unconditional is to know your supreme Father, your divine Mother, for the very nature of this universe is love, unconditional love.

Forgiveness

*"Forgiveness is the scent released by a violet
Upon the heel that has just crushed it."*
UNKNOWN ORIGIN

The concept of forgiveness is spoken of in many spiritual traditions. In Biblical terms, it is said that we should turn the other cheek, have gentle behavior and practice nonviolence. To be able to do this, you must be able to forgive the one who has affronted you or who has harmed you.

How do you practice forgiveness? Does it mean that if somebody does an ill act to you, that you merely accept it? This is not exactly the meaning of forgiveness. To forgive someone is to understand his or her suffering not to take it into you. Deepen your insight so that you can see the pain of another and how out of his or her suffering and pain, harsh acts toward you arose. Seeing this, you may realize that perhaps the ill action is even a cry for help. You see how different this is? Perhaps the person is crying for help like a little child screaming and throwing things because he or she doesn't know how to deal with the pain. The person needs help and so has attacked you out of ignorance and pain. If your mind goes deep enough, your empathy strong enough, you will see the very cause of the suffering.

Rather than take somebody's actions personally, you might apply an attitude of compassion. Perhaps you even contemplate how you can help. Having compassion for living beings, their pain and the harsh actions that come from their pain, is the root of forgiveness. When you move into a place of completeness governed by love, compassion and knowledge, then no ill act of another will harm you, for you will not take it into yourself. This ability comes from maturity of mind. The idea of forgiveness is a little glimpse, the beginning of a state of mind where compassion dominates you. This is a state where you are complete in your Self, complete in your divine nature, where nothing and no one can harm you. You see only the need and you act accordingly.

If you or those you love have been badly harmed by the actions of another, forgiveness may be difficult to achieve. You may struggle with desires for revenge, for justice, for the situation to be made right somehow. Yet this does not always happen and injustices do occur in the world. When all is said and done and the dust settles, we are left with how we can best cope with the hurt, the pain and the sense of injustice that remains when harm has been done. Feelings of helplessness, despair, anger and rage can occur.

FORGIVENESS IS GIVING SPACE THROUGH ACCEPTANCE OF WHAT WE CANNOT CHANGE.

The problem then is not the aggressor or oppressor, but how to heal ourselves and find our peace and happiness again. This is where forgiveness comes into play. It is a kind of letting go, making ourselves large enough to embrace even that which is so intolerable and find our joy and the brightness of love again. To do this we need to let go of our enmeshment with the perpetrator of the harm.

Forgiveness is the way we loosen his or her hold on us. Forgiveness is giving space through acceptance of what we cannot change and compassion for even the darker aspects of human experience until again the light of the inner Self shines bright in the mind and love returns. Then slowly, slowly light fills the darkness and we let go of our mental entanglement with the one who has done the harm. Seeing the pain of the perpetrator, having compassion and letting go, we begin to rebuild. We find love, awaken spirit and begin to realize how strong the human heart really is. This process starts with forgiveness, letting go and being with what is. This practice of compassion for all those who have hurt us so deeply allows us to heal.

If someone is offering an affront or doing harm to you, when you do not take the individual's actions personally and practice forgiveness, then you tend not to hold on to the experience. However, when the hurtful action or the affront is taken personally, you will react with anger, you will react with hurt. You will be wounded. If you take it to heart, it will harm you. If instead, you do not take it to heart, it will roll off like water off a duck's back. Forgiveness comes when you are able not to take to heart the affronts or wrongdoings of others toward you. When you begin to see that they are in reaction to their own pain and suffering and that their affront or actions against you were not meant personally toward you, it becomes easier to have a little distance. You become able to be unreactive, untouched by the behavior of others and thus maintain your equanimity of mind.

You can let go because you are untouched by the ill action. However, the question then comes, what if the person continues to do the affront or the harm to you? What if his or her actions are even harming other people? Then what to do? If someone continues to do ill actions toward you or toward others, then action may be needed to stop him or her, not out of anger, not out of reaction, but in practical steps to contain the damage that will be done or is being done by the individual's actions. Forgiveness is not simply to accept and allow all type of negative behaviors but is the ability to let go of your own reactivity, your own tendency to take the actions of others personally.

Samskaras, your subconscious reactions to different experiences you have had, form when the reactive mind is activated. When you stay in balance and you do not take the hurts and ill actions of others toward you to heart, then the reactions of mind become minimal. The impact on you is not there. You maintain yourself in loving kindness and compassion. This, like all of the ethical understandings of spiritual life, leads to a certain equanimity of mind, a peacefulness of mind that allows for knowledge of the Divine.

FORGIVENESS COMES WHEN YOU ARE ABLE NOT TO TAKE TO HEART THE AFFRONTS OR WRONGDOINGS OF OTHERS TOWARD YOU.

Practicing forgiveness helps you clear away distress. This enables you to have the calm needed to focus your mind and sink into your meditation practice without difficulty. Having forgiveness and compassion, selfless acts of kindness arise. When you are seeing the Divine everywhere, detachment emerges. These bring you the ability to maneuver the weals and woes of the world with minimal distress and find your way to love.

Gratitude

There are some whose lives are filled with great blessings but still feel that they have nothing. And there are those who are truly poor, yet given even the slightest crumb will feel they are most fortunate. One may be as wealthy as a prince or princess and still feel impoverished or as poor as the poorest beggar and feel wealthy. The feeling in the mind is not dictated by the external circumstances or environment but by the mental approach taken by the individual.

When you want to be happy, to make the best of your life, it is best to take the approach of the person who feels that whatever they have, be it great or be it ever so humble is the blessing of God. It is better to feel that you are fortunate than to feel you are deprived. Either feeling might be there, be you rich or be you poor, be you overflowing with opportunities or be you lacking in direction.

The practice of gratitude can take many forms. You may begin with simple exercises such as beginning and ending each day by remembering or even writing down all the things you are grateful for. They can be large or small, from a new job you are excited about to a flower you saw blooming by the side of the road, a beautiful sunset or a person who smiled at you warmly in a store. Part of the practice of gratitude is simply beginning to notice all the good things that go on around you each and every day. Sometimes we get conditioned only to notice what is wrong with the world and our lives and we overlook what is right. Gratitude is turning that process around.

SOMETIMES WE GET CONDITIONED ONLY TO NOTICE WHAT IS WRONG WITH THE WORLD.

Another helpful practice is to remember all the kind deeds done toward you by others. Think of someone you know and appreciate and express your gratitude. Write him a letter or email or even better tell him in person how much you appreciate him. Notice what others do well and express your appreciation. And don't forget your animal friends and plants. Notice what they give and appreciate them also. When you live in appreciation of life and reverence for life you become alive, vibrant in gratitude and joy.

When you cultivate a positive outlook and an approach that is appreciative of all that you are given, of everything that you have in your life, you will be a happy person. Whatever you have, be it ever so humble, do not compare yourself to others you believe have more than you or assume through comparison that you are impoverished. This is not a good approach to life. There is always someone who has more than you when you take this outlook. This hungry ghost can never be satiated.

Instead of becoming a hungry ghost, the better approach is to notice what you are blessed with, all the people, living beings and things in your life that you are fortunate to have around you. Even the simple things of life can become the blessings of God, for in fact, they are the blessings of God. It is only the deficiency of the mind when you cannot perceive what you are given. It is best to feel that whatever you have is grace and to feel grateful. Cultivate the feeling that you are a most fortunate person and that you are cared for by your supreme Father, your divine Mother. Cultivate the feeling that you are given grace in your life.

In so many ways, the divine Being is supporting you, in your experience, your development, even in your pain, even in your difficulty you are being supported. When a child makes mistakes, the results provide life lessons. From the negative results, the child learns to pursue a different road that will be more effective. Even when you are prevented from going forward in a desired direction, it may be the grace of the Divine that is opening another direction that will lead you where you really need to go. For the Divine looks at your heart and seeing your heart will help you go where you must go to become all that you can be. So do not be unhappy with your life; do not be sad with your existence for your future is bright and the Divine looks after you with great love and affection.

So, gratitude is not only in what you do but how you approach what you do. If you take the view that whatever is given to you in life is a blessing, you will find that your life is filled with blessings throughout. You will find that you have much potential within that will evolve forward as time goes on.

WHEN YOU LIVE IN APPRECIATION OF LIFE AND REVERENCE FOR LIFE, YOU BECOME ALIVE, VIBRANT IN GRATITUDE AND JOY.

Never be disheartened; never allow yourself to be discouraged; know that you are guided. The same force that guides the stars guides you also. That which is in the depths of your heart is what you really need to find your way home to the ocean of love. The Source will come to you and guide you, for grace surrounds you. So live in gratitude. Live in reverence for life and transform your life in joyous appreciation.

Compassion

People tend to emulate others, but who, or what traits, a person emulates makes all the difference. If you focus on emulating the qualities and characteristics of the Divine, then you move toward love and compassion. For the Divine is the source of compassion.

When you develop compassion, you put real love into practice. Seeing the pain and suffering of others, your heart goes out with compassion to help them. You are not thinking of what you can get out of the situation or even how it will impact you. Your concern is what is needed to help or heal and how you can make that happen. Compassion involves empathy, an ability to relate to the pain of others, to feel it, to know it and to care that someone is experiencing it. Oftentimes, people who have been through a great deal of suffering themselves are the ones who develop this kind of empathy, an ability to really understand the suffering of others and truly care. The result of facing your own suffering and working with it is that you become able to accept the suffering of others, understand their pain and care. This is compassion.

THE RESULT OF FACING YOUR OWN SUFFERING AND WORKING WITH IT IS THAT YOU BECOME ABLE TO ACCEPT THE SUFFERING OF OTHERS.

Compassion, as a practice, requires you to face your own pain and the pain and suffering that exists in this world without looking away. It requires you to be able to be with suffering, to see it and those who suffer with great love, great care. Compassion is an attitude, a feeling, a reflection of all embracing, unconditional love. It holds nothing back and doesn't run. The practice of compassion must start with yourself, with facing your own pain and having great kindness for the part of yourself that has suffered. Then you can take that same care and share your heart with all beings in the loving kindness of compassion.

Begin by treating others as you would be treated, with kindness. Do not covet what they have. Make efforts to care for their needs in a kind and compassionate way. This does not mean that you need to bow to the wishes of every person who wants something from you. This is not compassion. Compassion is to be kind and to care about the needs of every living being. When in an attitude of compassion, all that you do is for the welfare of living beings. It is a kindness that you express in your daily life. If you live in this kindness you will find that there is a significant effect on other people and on yourself.

When you learn to see everything as the manifestation of God and treat all people and all life with utmost respect, the world around you becomes the very expression of divinity. As you develop your awareness with the practice of *Yama* and *Niyama*, you begin to acquire positive qualities and characteristics within yourself, and the compassionate nature of the infinite *Brahma* begins to be reflected in your mind and personality. If you are doing these practices, how can you help but have understanding and great care for the depth of suffering that exists in this world, not only for human beings but for those in animal form, for all living beings? When you see the beautiful nature of each and every living being and the suffering that abounds, you cannot help but develop a heart of great compassion.

Loving Your Own Self

Loving yourself is essential because it is by loving your own self that you become able to love others. When you learn to view your own faults and failings with understanding and compassion, you become able to accept and love others, even when you know their imperfections. When you see divinity in your own being you become able to see the divine in others. The attitudes and approaches you develop toward others begin with the feelings you have about your own self.

If you can love all parts of yourself and accept yourself fully, then you can have compassion for others. Love Divine does not discriminate, does not pick and choose. It is love unconditional. When love for your own self becomes unconditional, when you can forgive yourself for all the ways you have not lived up to how you think you should be, then you become able to touch Love Divine. Your own personality as well as your body, mind and sense of self are all expressions of the one eternal Self. When you love yourself and all beings, you love the divine in manifest form. Within you are shadows and light, joys and pain. When you hold all parts of yourself equally with acceptance and love, you move into balance. From that balance comes the deep meditative harmony with divine Consciousness, divine Essence. In that harmony, oneness exists. There, the love you have been seeking can be found. There, you find the wholeness that dissolves all suffering.

THE ATTITUDES AND APPROACHES YOU DEVELOP TOWARD OTHERS BEGIN WITH THE FEELINGS YOU HAVE ABOUT YOUR OWN SELF.

Know that each and every person, including you, is unconditionally loved, unconditionally cared for. There is no sin you have committed, no crime you have done that will outcast you from the love of *Parama Brahma*. That love is like a gently falling rain, a shower of grace. It is only when you are afraid, holding up the umbrella of ego, afraid to let it down, afraid to let love in, that this love cannot be felt. When you let it down and let love in, the love that is there is vast and unconditioned. You are the dear child of the beloved One. When you feel that, you know you are never alone, and you will never again be alone, for the Divine is always with you.

You are always cherished. This guidance, this shower of grace, of unconditional love is always there, always. It is only when you are looking away and absorbed with all of the details of your life that the defensiveness of *I and mine* comes. Due to your distracted attention, divine love becomes invisible. It is always there, only you do not hear the sweet small voice within. You do not see the shower of grace. You become deaf; you become blind; all you see are separate forms that come and go.

When you awaken, then the eyes open. The true Guru is the one who applies the ointment of knowledge and removes the darkness from your eyes. By grace you may see, hear and know love, know truth. When you experience loneliness, take the shelter of your most Beloved and know that you are always loved, unconditionally. Feel that shower of grace surround you and know that you are not alone. That loving consciousness, that infinite, caressing, caring intelligence permeates all that is. Everyone you have loved is an expression of that. You have seen the Beloved in the eyes of those you have loved, your children, your spouse, your lover. You have seen the Divine in their eyes.

See that One in your own heart. Feel the grace around you. Let go of the encasement around your heart. Let go of the duality of *I and mine*. Let go of your fear and your separation. Sink into the Beloved. Feel the grace. This is yours. It will always be yours. It never changes. The love of the Infinite is unconditional, always with you every moment of every day, with you when you came into this world, with you when you leave, with you in your hardest times, with you in your greatest joy. You are guided, protected and loved unconditionally.

Know this love. It is in your own heart-cave. This love belongs to you. This One is the Self of yourself, your source, your home. The aching in every human heart is to end the experience of duality and to be united with the whole of being again, to return home to the sea of love from which all have come. This is your birthright. It is your natural state, *sahaj*. This is true self-love.

CHAPTER V

Facing the Shadow

Instinct and Ethics

The question arises, is ethical truth universal? Or are ethical practices such as *Yama* and *Niyama* relative, dependent on who is interpreting them and their perspective? It is said that those who win wars write history, and according to their version of history, it is determined who the moral party was and who was the immoral aggressor. If this is the case, are there any standards of human behavior that transcend personal or group perspectives, or is it all open to interpretation? This question has deep ramifications.

Instinct Versus Ethics

One must ask oneself, what is morality? Do ethical principles ever transcend the relative perspective of a particular group? When there were feudal kingdoms, it was one kingdom against another and each thought it had the righteous cause. With nations and wars, it is the same; one group against another, each feeling it has the righteous cause, the good purpose for which it will spend the lives of its citizens.

In a world where two different groups feel justified in their superior moral stance, both feel that God is on their side, where does truth stand?

You cannot turn to history because the victors write the histories. You cannot ask one side or the other; they will both tell you that theirs is the

WHAT WAR IS FOUGHT THAT BOTH SIDES DO NOT HAVE GRIEVOUS LOSSES?

right side. In terms of atrocities and ill behavior, both sides will offer examples of the ill behavior of the other side. What war is fought that both sides do not have grievous losses and claims of ill behavior on the part of the other? Wars can be large-scale between multiple countries on each side or they can be family feuds between one family and another, between one group and another or even between two individuals. The same dynamics apply.

In the ancient traditions of yogic thought, *Yama* and *Niyama* give recommendations for human behavior. In Christianity, the Ten Commandments also give codes for behavior. Muslims also have codes. There are codes of conduct in all societies. They are usually taken very seriously except when it comes to the interests of the country, the kingdom, the king, the party, the group; then they become challenged.

In Christianity, one of the fundamental codes is, "Thou shalt not kill" and yet it was the Christian church behind the Crusades, the Inquisition, the witch-hunts. Those pious people felt justified in their actions, that they were doing the right thing even though they were killing people, violating their own commandments. Despite the contradiction with their own code of conduct, the people acting for the church in these situations thought their actions under the circumstances were justified because the situation was different. The people they killed were infidels, pagans, unholy. These groups did not espouse to the true religion. Therefore, the church felt justified in the actions. Similarly in today's world, extremist Muslim sects support the random killing of innocents despite the guidance of the *Quran,* because the victims are considered infidels. They are not of the true faith. Therefore the killings are justified.

When taking a step back and observing human behavior within group situations, you might ask yourself, "Why is this pattern there?" You can justify it or explain it as extremist behavior. However, violent actions are not limited to extremist sects. Devout Hindus will go to the village of Muslims and kill men, women and children then go back to the temple and pray feeling justified in their actions. Average people find themselves in diverse situations in which violence is condoned.

Throughout history, different groups, warring clans, families, nations have done terrible things to each other. The ones who are defeated are murdered, raped, conquered and must submit. You might think that the people doing such actions do not have an ethical code like *Yama* and *Niyama* but most groups have codes. Or you might think of such groups as extremist or aberrant or unusual but this doesn't really address the scope of the issue. In fact, if you look at the history of human beings, this aggression toward the other and the justification of aggressive and harmful acts are both very common.

Once a person is well-established in identity with a group, it is very easy to classify another group as immoral and your own as moral. The group that affronts your group, seeks to acquire something that you have or demonstrates other behaviors that do not support your society becomes the enemy. Remember one of the guidelines of *Yama* is *Asteya*, not to covet or steal from another. Yet the reality is that in social groups, the expansion of territory and *THE DESIRE TO THRIVE AND* the desire to have more wealth, *SURVIVE IS THE STRUGGLE OF* food, well-being and security *HUMAN LIFE.* will naturally bring one group in conflict with another unless there is a great deal of free land. When conflicts happen, there is a clash between the groups, clans, tribes or societies. Then one group will attempt to dominate the other. It will attempt to bring the ideology of its people forward and to have the people of the other group submit to its rule.

So you see, terrorist groups promote the ideology of their cult. They condemn the perceived enemy as immoral and they can surely recount endless failures in the behaviors of the other. They submit to the beliefs of the group and then act accordingly, feeling their actions are noble.

These terrorist groups are not alone in their psychology, though they may be more violent in their actions than some. They act much as many other societies do. However some societies are a little more sophisticated in how they present their aggressive actions.

As long as one group is against another, conflict or war is inevitable. When the people of one country are at war with another, their loved ones have been hurt and their minds are bitter with the pain of loss. They feel aggression toward the other side. They want to hurt the enemy as they have been hurt. The people of the other country feel injustice was done to them and they feel pain for their loved ones and they also want to hurt the other. Both sides feel they are right. Both feel they are justified. Both feel that truth and righteousness are on their side. This is the deception, the illusion.

IT IS THE INSTINCTUAL TENDENCIES OF THE ANIMAL BODIES OF HUMAN BEINGS THAT ARE THE ROOT CAUSE OF THE VIOLENT TENDENCIES OF GROUPS.

Justification of aggressive acts can become the norm. It may seem that ethics, whether governed by the Ten Commandments, *Yama* and *Niyama* or other ethical codes are relative, as surely their application often seems to be. However, despite the struggles people face in applying these codes, there seem to be essential ethical principles that transcend groups, winners, losers and sides.

If people could avoid identification with groups and thus engagement in harmful group actions, this might solve the aggression issue. This appears to be simple to do but it is not so simple because people's instinctual tendencies drive them to join group actions. It is the instinctual tendencies of the animal bodies of human beings that are the root cause of the violent tendencies of groups and thus wars.

Instincts

It is easy to look at bears and tigers and deer to see the behaviors of their species but human beings are much less inclined to look at their own instincts. Human beings have survived by being part of a group, clan, family, tribe. Survival of human beings has depended upon group identity. And in the instinctual relationships within a human clan, tribe or family there is hierarchy. As the wolves have a hierarchy within packs, so humans have a hierarchy in their clans or tribes. It is instinctual to follow the dominant leader. Why? Survival. Those clans with a strong leader who have the capacity of protection of the group are the ones who have survived.

Human beings tend to attach themselves to a strong leader then to accept whatever is given as the group norm and to believe it wholeheartedly. This behavior has one moral code, survival. That is the morality of these instinctual behaviors. It is a morality that puts survival above any other standard. If one must kill to maintain the dominance of one's group, expand the territory of one's group, increase the food supply or the assets of one's group, to insure the procreation of one's group, then it is acceptable because behavior is governed by fears around survival.

In all human cultures, spiritual leaders who are connected to the Divine have made efforts to mitigate this survival instinct and the behaviors that result from it by encouraging standards of ethics. They have established guidelines that give standards for compassion and kindness, encouraging principles such as not to kill, treat others with kindness, be honest and truthful, refrain from taking from others. These types of guidelines are common across different cultures because they are given from the Higher Self. They encourage behaviors that support unitary awareness and the more developed expressions of human behavior. These higher standards are ever at war with the instinctual tendencies within human beings and human societies.

Instincts tend to dominate the minds of people in unconscious ways. They are so much a part of the human psyche that most people barely notice when their instincts are taking over. Often people do not notice them because survival behaviors are ascribed positive attributes within the group or society and aggressive acts are justified. The values that sustain the survival and expansion of a clan, tribe, society or nation are not the values that have been given for the people in the commandments from the Divine to the sages and saints. The values or ethics given by the holy ones are not relative. They may appear relative due to their interpretations within different societies and people's self-justifications. However the standards themselves are not relative.

What is relative is the capacity of people to understand the standards and to follow them. People become blinded by the instinct to follow the herd and accept the prevailing social norms. Accepting the beliefs of the group and supporting them become paramount. This is so dominant that most people do not realize how it is affecting them. They simply take it for granted.

Dominance, Submission, Instinct and Survival

Dominant and submissive behaviors occur in all strata of society because they are part of the human instinct for survival. To submit to power, to be dominant where there is weakness, to establish territory are all expressions of our instinct. Even sacrificing your life for your nation, religion or another primary group can be part of human survival behaviors, as our instincts are not only aimed at individual survival but focus upon the survival of the society as well. In fact the group's survival may be even more important than the individual's survival. Throughout history, a strong tribe, clan or society has been necessary to assure survival of self and offspring. Without it, people have often not survived. Identity of the individual with the group for prosperity and personal survival is part of our genetics. When this identity is strong, the group welfare comes first.

When one separates oneself from all of the normal prejudices of one's society; when one stands apart from one's group with a calm mind, it can be seen how in all strata of human endeavor, people operate by instinctual patterns. The patterns of dominance and submission are prevalent in all societies, even in families. From birth, they are ingrained in children. They arise in how we relate to issues such as gender, being first-born or last-born. They determine whether the child is cultivated to be dominant or submissive. All the circumstances of the society reinforce these patterns to create a cohesive group or social order.

These instinctual patterns of behavior go into family systems, churches, schools, into all groups where people have an identity with the group. The stronger the group identity, the more submission to group values will show up. This is the reality and no group is above it. The desire to thrive and survive is the struggle of human life and the dynamics of power are the dynamics of human society.

Working with Violence and Harm

War is still prevalent in human society and when people disagree, they may do great harm to others. To varying degrees, depending on the society and the circumstance, this may be socially acceptable. When violence is condoned, it is not uncommon for violence to occur collectively – violence of gangs, mobs and wars. All collective violence is rooted in the acceptance of violence.

Violence also occurs in the relationships of men and women; physical and psychic violence against women is still common. In some countries, the law still approves of physical violence by a man toward his wife. A man living in such a culture may feel quite comfortable to do harm mentally or physically to his wife. The society around him condones and supports the behavior and, as a result, he may feel quite justified and morally correct in violent actions toward her.

IT IS TO COUNTER THESE VIOLENT AND SELF-CENTERED TENDENCIES THAT THE VALUES OF YAMA AND NIYAMA HAVE BEEN GIVEN.

Does this mean that *Yama* and *Niyama* are bendable because in his society violence against woman is acceptable, that he does not violate *Yama* and *Niyama*? If he does meditation and attempts to lead an ethical life, though the society may condone his action, hopefully due to his meditation practice, he will realize this is not right action, despite social approval.

To harm another physically or mentally is not right action. Yet I do not think there is a single person who will read this who has not done harm to another to one degree or another. In the conflicts and struggles of human beings, harm occurs in so many situations. In the conflicts and struggles of human beings, jealousies occur. In the conflicts and struggles of human beings, revenges occur. In the conflicts and struggles between human beings, the desire to take from another to secure oneself occurs.

It is to counter these violent and self-centered tendencies that the values of *Yama and Niyama* have been given. You can become aware through meditation and reflection on the ethical principles of how you might have harmed others. Thus, you may make every effort to cease from such actions, to have compassion for others, to have forgiveness. It does not mean that you allow others to victimize you. However, while standing strong against any type of violence or victimization that is directed toward you, remember to keep your heart and mind free from hatred, anger and revengeful feelings.

Have compassion for those who have difficulty with their own tendencies and do your best to assist them gently to improve. This assistance may come in different ways. It may come through a gentle approach but if they refuse to stop the action, then the approach may need to become stronger and if still they refuse to listen, then strong action may be needed to stop harmful actions.

Harm is always relative. Harm will be done at one time or another, if not in action, then in intention or in thought. The more subtle the environment or the individual, the more subtle the realms of harm can become. The more crude the person is, the more crude and obviously violent the harm, but either way significant progress is made when the individual attempts to rectify the harmful action and moves to a greater degree of love and compassion.

In this physical world there is struggle. There is life. There is death. There are the hunters and the hunted, the cat and the deer. Yet, in your ethics always avoid harm to living beings. Never indulge in aggression yourself but stand strong against that which is not life supporting. Stand for truth. Stand for love. Stand for compassion and care for all living beings. Treat all beings as if they are the very Lord come before you. There is no one to hate in this world for the Infinite is in all forms, even those of the most despicable people who have done the greatest harm to living beings. But this does not mean that you let them continue to harm others. No, you stop them. And you yourself do not engage in harm.

Right and Wrong Actions

An action done by one person may seem unethical to another observing it or to someone on the receiving end of the action, but to the person doing the action it may seem moral and justified. Where do *dharma* and right action lie? Recommendations for right actions are given in the *Yama* and *Niyama* and definitions of *dharma* (the way toward the Divine) are given but all is subject to interpretation. What does it mean to steal from another? A person losing something they value to another may say that an action of the other person was a theft but the person taking something may not feel it is actually a theft. They may feel it is justified and, in fact, they may believe the object does not belong to the person they took it from. One may say that an action is harmful because one person experiences it as hurtful or painful. However the person doing the harmful act may think it is an appropriate response to the other person's actions. So where does truth lie in this? Is it only the perspective of the individual that matters?

Naturally, in this relative world, time, place and person make a difference in understanding right action. What may be an ethical activity in one age may be an act of cruelty and destruction in another age. In a hot country, eating any type of flesh of an animal can be considered not only a cruel action but also unhealthy. In a cold climate where there is ice and no vegetables, nothing to eat but the flesh of animals, the same action ceases to be considered unhealthy and eating the meat becomes a necessity. The harm done to a living being is the same; still the circumstance makes a difference in the values surrounding the action.

Values change as society changes. As a society becomes more subtle, its standards rise. There is only one absolute truth and that is the infinite Divinity, the one eternal consciousness that is ever omnipresent and unchanging.

This created universe is relative and holds a diversity of experience from what can only be called hell realms to heaven realms of bliss and sweetness. This earth plane lies neither in hell nor in heaven, but struggle is a part of this earthly plane. They say that the *yogis*, to finish the process of enlightenment, must take birth in this physical world, that one cannot attain full Self-realization from the heaven realms. Though one may attain by good karma a birth in heavenly realms, one must come to this earthly plane to attain full realization.

This is because it is in this realm that the play of duality exists in full and one is challenged to transmute and transcend the crude to the subtle. The full spectrum of opportunity for the worst of lives and the best of lives, for the worst of *ALL IS DEPENDENT ON TIME, PLACE AND PERSON.* actions and the best of actions exists in this realm. So it is in this realm that all are challenged to see through the veil of ignorance and to seek the ever more subtle and divine.

All is dependent on time, place and person. The witnessing individual consciousness, the particular society, the particular set of experiences all come into play. The world is relative. Perception is relative. Values are relative. Yet within this relativity, there are norms. There are standards.

There are actions that lead toward Divinity, toward knowledge of the Divine and actions that lead away. Even in the realm of relativity, though actions are relative there is directional flow. If a person lives in a crude society and is trained to rough habits, then when that person shows even the smallest kindness or fights against violent and crude tendencies they are moving toward the light. Even by showing the smallest compassion, some ethical awareness, some desire for truth, then that person has moved toward Divinity. The path of *dharma*, movement toward truth, is followed. However, the same set of actions done by someone in a refined society, with ample opportunity to understand ethical behavior, could be considered crude and bring the person away from Divinity. They would be *adharmic*, moving away from the path to truth.

Which actions are considered right or wrong may vary according to time, place and person. The direction to which the actions move the mind and heart of an individual is of significance. This is what determines if it is really a right action. Today's world is different than the world of ten-thousand years ago, of twenty-thousand years ago, fifty-thousand years ago and it will be different in the world of one-thousand years from now.

Be Your Own Person

For most people, when the group goes one way, they go that way; they believe what the group believes. When the group goes another way, they go that way. Why? Because they have surrendered to the group psychology, as their instincts around power and submission tell them to do for their survival.

Human beings are not so strong; have compassion for them. Just as the wolf has an instinctual response within its society or the deer with its herd, or the horses, or the birds, so human beings are equally bound in their reactions. People in general have a profound mental pride that they do not see their responses to their own societies. They do not see how they are giving away their ability to make personal choices to the groups they identify with.

THE TRUE SPIRITUAL SEEKER FOLLOWS THE DIVINE AND NOT ANY GROUP, NOT ANY EXTERNAL FORCE.

Instinctual survival and group behaviors are in the genes

but for the true *yogi* who has a personal association with God, in the process of meditation, as the higher layers of mind open, these genes lose their influence. As one grows toward an enlightened state, the genes that create these instincts and the survival needs that drive behaviors of dominance become less and less active and eventually turn off. Then love for the Supreme dominates.

The *yogi* who wants to know truth must step apart from this biology, from the dominance of the body and the way the body structures the mind. To do this, begin to witness your own existence. As higher layers of the mind become accessible, the calm witness, knowledge and detachment from the animal instincts grows. Instincts are driven by fear and all that happens as a result of them is based in fear. The closer you are to the Divine, the more the instincts of survival turn off and the fear that drives them dissolves.

All those who teach about this problem give the same advice: Avoid group identification. Feel that the whole universe is your home; all living beings your children, your family. Stand apart from any side and take actions of loving kindness and compassion. Seeing the pain and the shortcomings of all people in this world, have compassion for the humanity, the difficulty, the struggle, the pain. Bring healing to humanity; approach all with compassion and love.

If you want this change, follow *Yama* and *Niyama*, rather than the dynamics of power and look very closely at your own self. Find your own relationship with the eternal Self and with all beings. You can only do this as an individual. The *samgha* (spiritual community) can help to a degree but it is important to have your eyes open when relating to a group to bring your internal locus of surrender where you give your power freely to the God within. The true spiritual seeker turns within to the Divine and seeks guidance from that one and not any external force.

Standards of morality need to come from your relationship to the Divine. Then there is a certain detachment from all groups and all group-isms. To avoid *DISCRIMINATIVE* group identity is much more difficult *UNDERSTANDING* and involved than it appears but it is *WILL CLARIFY ISSUES.* key to being able to follow *Yama* and *Niyama*. So have all the Masters taught. Essential morality does not lie within a group psychology. It lies within you as an individual and within your relationship to the God Self. And that relationship is personal and singular.

The true *Sadvipra* (developed spiritual person) is a part of all groups and a part of none. Being a person who stands for *dharma*, he or she lives by ethics, for the love of the Divine. Actions are governed by personal experience and by what has been revealed from the innermost being.

Understanding Conflict

The Masters say, "Have love for all beings; do no harm to others; do not try to acquire what is not yours; be truthful and be honest." Deep honesty comes as we grow closer to the one eternal Self and higher layers of the mind are activated. Deep truthfulness and self-honesty are great steps toward the activation of the yogic capacity of true discrimination, awakened in subtle layers of being.

Without this discriminative understanding, it is difficult for people to consider conflict objectively. To understand human conflict requires deep inquiry into the source of the conflict and an ability to hold the duality. Significant investigation is needed into the underlying perceptions, and positions, as well as *YOU NEED TO BE IN THE* the source of those perceptions, *WORLD BUT NOT OF IT.* in order to know where a positive and happy resolution might be found in a conflict. Too much intellectual speculation may cloud the issue. Discriminative understanding will clarify issues. When you step apart and connect to the Self within, you can establish a sense of *dharma* for yourself and will be able to take the enlightened view that all beings are your family, your children.

Then suddenly the differences between people begin to fade. It can be perceived that all people are doing the same thing. They are all trying to secure themselves, to feel safe, to have their needs met, to survive. You see in the deer that the bucks will attack each other with their antlers, lock antlers and fight to the death. Why? Instinct drives them. They have a lot at stake. Human beings feel the same and in certain situations they also may have a lot at stake.

Understanding behavior in groups is not a matter of knowing who is right and who is wrong. Belief in right and wrong sides is part of the problem. The solution involves learning how to stand apart, to be inner-directed, taking the divine Source as your polestar, as the one to whom you surrender everything, taking all the beings of the universe as part of your own family and then adhering to the deeper ethics expressed in practices such as *Yama* and *Niyama*.

Then you begin to see that there is not so much difference between one group and another. You stand with eyes open, without judgment, with a neutrality of mind, observing the suffering in human life and the happiness. This reflective consciousness is needed to really be able to follow *Yama* and *Niyama*. No one is an island. Human beings need each other. We need to feel we are part of something, something great. It is inherent in the human body. Being a part of something is the way we survive but there is also a deep longing within to return to wholeness. When the need to be a part of something is focused upon the Divine rather than a specific group, then we become a part of the greater whole. We open up the avenue to find our real shelter in the storm of life. We become a part of all the groups. We walk within the society but we are not of the society. We love all and feel with great compassion the human condition.

THE YOGI WHO WANTS TO KNOW TRUTH MUST STEP APART FROM THIS BIOLOGY.

It takes great awareness and great compassion to look at the world a little bit differently, with kindness, compassion and understanding for all societies, all groups, all elements within any society. When you really step aside from your own group identity, then you open up the possibility to see and feel yourself as a part of all groups in the societies.

Incorporating Yama and Niyama

Divinity is everywhere, in everyone. The Divine does not take sides. In the wars of the world, an awake person is not

Russian or American, is not a Serb or of any race, any nation, any group. He or she identifies with all groups, regardless or origin. *Yama* and *Niyama* will lead a person closer to this knowledge; that all are part of one whole and the tendency of dividing, focusing on differences and struggles one against another, is not the truth of life.

Yama and *Niyama* are paths to the application of truth. Connection to God is not an excuse for righteous aggression. Compassion, knowledge of the unity of all beings and understanding of the relativity of perspective leads to right action. For there is only one perspective from which true acts of great compassion arise and that is the knowledge that all beings, *PUT ASIDE IDEAS OF RIGHT AND WRONG AND GOOD AND BAD IN FAVOR OF LOVE.* from the smallest ant to the greatest most powerful leader, are the embodiment of the one eternal Self. Even the most despicable tyrant and the angelic saint are both the embodiment of the eternal Self.

So put aside ideas of right and wrong and good and bad in favor of love. Then you will be able to find your way to the right application of *dharma* and truth. You will be able to find your way to loving kindness and true strength.

This world is not perfect. Human life is not perfect. Do your best to attach your instinctual tendencies to the divine flow of infinite love. Looking within, attach your life to the Divine. Then that One will guide you. Make the whole of all living beings your family. If you have children of your own and some are getting into mischief, you still love them. With your own children, you have kind feelings for them, even if they are the troublemakers. You understand the pain that drives them. Think of all beings, thus, as your very own children.

By following *Yama* and *Niyama* to the best of your ability and avoiding group identification, you can move toward opening higher layers of the mind. When higher layers of the mind open, instincts break down and true knowledge comes. Embracing *Yama* and *Niyama* as a way of life, the mind grows in magnitude; your knowledge of truth expands and then there is greater detachment and more autonomy. Exploring instincts and ethics challenges the basic assumptions you are conditioned to. Everything has taught you to follow conditioned responses, but these do not relate to the practices of *Yama* and *Niyama*.

CHAPTER VI

Healing the Mind

"How can you look so needy,
God is growing in fields you own.
He hangs from trees you pass by every day.
He is disguised as that peach and pine cone.
Every sound I hear – He made it."

RUMI

Working with Our Emotions and The Struggles in Our Lives

There are times in every person's life when personal difficulties arise in one form or another. These difficulties can cause a person to feel despondent, even discouraged. If the issues are overwhelming, or the circumstances really difficult, a person may become extremely discouraged and experience much distress. In yogic practices, it is *Yama* and *Niyama* that address these human struggles. In particular, the practices of *Niyama* are important in changing how we relate to ourselves. Many of the concepts covered in this chapter have been discussed elsewhere but are explored here in relationship to psychological healing.

When psychological issues arise, practicing *Yama* and *Niyama* helps to relieve despondency, stress, strain and mental difficulties because these practices address our attitudes, understandings and behaviors, empowering us to move forward to a healthier paradigm.

When you practice *Saucha*, a pure mind, a pure heart, devoid of complicated motivations, begins to develop. When you practice *Santosha*, contentment with life becomes a possibility; the potential of a positive sense of acceptance and peace with what is arises.

THERE IS BEAUTY BOTH IN THE STORMS OF LIFE AND BEAUTY IN THE SUNNY DAYS.

When you accept yourself as you are and what life brings to you as it is, you are in a position to heal the mind and body because there is acceptance of the totality of your experience. There is beauty in the storms of life and beauty in the sunny days. The storms are needed to bring the waters that sustain life and the sun is needed to bring the life energy and light that allows life to grow and expand. Both are necessary in the cycles of nature and of our lives.

In the cycles of human experience, sometimes it is a sunny day and sometimes it is a rainy day but both are a part of the growth, development and nurturing of life. Recognizing this through the daily practice of *Santosha*, cultivating acceptance and contentment, finding a sense of well-being and peace of mind with life as it is opens up possibilities in your life.

Incorporating this practice allows you to open to the experience of selfless love. Not only are peace, harmony and acceptance really possible in life, allowing you to appreciate the beauty of even the smallest joys, but cultivating awareness of yourself as part of a network of life becomes possible through selfless acts.

Learning through the practice of *Tapas* to relate to the world around you with kindness and to care for others, assisting them even though you have your own needs, opens the heart. When you assist living beings, you begin to realize the magnitude of the needs of others. You begin to see that you are not the only one with troubles in this world and to care about the suffering of others. By seeing the troubles that other people have and helping them, you become more able to help yourself. You become aware that you are part of an integrated whole of life and that your small existence is part of something more vast. Your identity changes and you begin to see yourself in all beings.

Then incorporating the practice of *Svadhyaya*, you not only read books of wisdom, attend talks, webinars, workshops and seminars on spiritual teachings, but you cultivate access to the wisdom that springs from within the deeper layers of your being. Accessing the wisdom of the true Self within, training the mind to right thinking avoids many problems. The mind, trailing off into distorted thinking gets confused. Difficult states of mind and emotions can arise from old patterns of thought. When you establish the mind in truth, in Love Divine, recognizing the truth of your own divine nature and the truth of love unconditional, then many of these disturbing thoughts and tendencies fade away.

Finally, through *Ishvara Pranidhana*, meditation upon the eternal One, surrendering everything you have been holding on to, all thoughts, ideas and concepts to the Divine; peace, calm and realization of the eternal nature of the Self can ensue. The Divine can take away all the thoughts that arise out of your identity with your individual existence and the related struggles and bring unconditional love to you. When you surrender all of your conditioned thinking to God, only the all-compassionate divine presence is left.

All these practices help the mind to gain clarity and balance. When there is purity of mind and heart from the practice of *Saucha*, purity of spirit follows and all distortions fly away. In this way the practices of *Niyama* bring the mind to a quiet and still state of self-surrender in which the true Self shines forth. The mind becomes balanced and in harmony with all life.

The practices of *Yama* also help to quiet distress in the mind. Practicing *Ahimsa* allows you to keep your thoughts about yourself and others compassionate and filled with loving-kindness. It encourages forgiveness and letting go of grudges, clearing away many pains and burdens. When you truly practice *Ahimsa*, you refrain from harmful and violent thoughts and actions, not only toward others but toward yourself. It allows you to see the connections between people. The pain and suffering of isolation in your ego begin to soften. For the benefit of all, it is best to have compassion for all living beings and practice forgiveness to those who have harmed you.

This does not mean to allow others to do harm to you or anyone else. It means do not react to their harmful actions with aggression. Rather, accept the flaws and failings of human beings, and accept your faults and failings as well. All beings are children of the Divine, part and parcel of the family of the Infinite.

To be truthful is difficult when the mind is clouded. *Satya* is not so easily practiced when the mind is distressed or disturbed because the mind generates all manner of difficult thoughts, resentful thoughts, hurtful thoughts, sad thoughts and worrisome thoughts. Amid all of these different thoughts, where is *Satya*? Distorted thinking abounds when the mind is disturbed. Thoughts, however pleasant, are not the source of truth. Truth lies in the one eternal Self.

THOUGHTS INCONSISTENT WITH THE NATURE OF THE ETERNAL SELF ARE NOT THE DEEPEST TRUTH.

Thoughts inconsistent with the nature of the eternal Self are not the deepest truth. Thoughts that recognize the Divinity in all beings, holding all with unconditioned love including yourself, bring you closer to truth. When you see the one eternal *Brahma* in all things, you abide in truth. When you engage in self-criticism, when you feel resentments, angers and hurts, when you feel that others have the power to harm you, you reside in only partial truths and the deeper truth evades you.

The eternal Self is omnipresent and omnipotent. The truth of that existence is eternal. Cling to that one alone and you will find safety and happiness. When all of your desires and activities become directed toward the infinite Self and all you encounter is seen as Divine, then your relationship to your existence shifts. A sometimes unpleasant and often mundane life can become transmuted into an experience of Divine bliss.

Practicing *Asteya*, not stealing or desiring what others have, also brings mental balance and not practicing it can bring psychological struggles. When there are difficulties in life, sometimes you may wish to be like someone else who you might admire. You project happiness, success and abundance on them that you may feel you do not have. If money is your issue, then you may think, "If I were rich like this person, then my life would be fine." If emotional struggles are your issue then you may think, "If only I were calm and peaceful like that person, then my life would be good. Then I could be happy." If loneliness is your issue, then you may think, "Oh, if only I had a partner like this other person, then my life would be good." Instead of practicing *Santosha* and finding the joy and harmony in your own existence, you begin to covet, to desire and to think that somebody else has it better than you. You begin to think that only if you had what they have, then your life would be good. When you feel this, resentment comes in the mind. Resentment that they have something you do not. Anger arises and out of anger and resentment, perhaps mean thoughts and even aggressive actions.

To practice *Asteya* is more complicated than simply not stealing property or identity from others. It has a subtle psychological form. Not stealing implies not wanting what others have. Thinking someone else has more than you – more friends, more social skills, more money, more power, more prestige and more happiness and therefore desiring what they have, leads to unhappiness about your own situation.

When the mind flows along these lines, *Asteya* is broken. When you really want what another has, there is a subtle desire to take from them, to steal, even if it is only in the mental sphere. This means there is a feeling of lack inside yourself; somehow what you are is not good enough. What you have or are is not good enough so peace within you, *Santosha,* is lost and *Satya* is broken because it is not the truth; you are good enough as you are. You are an expression *YOU ARE PROVIDED FOR IN SO MANY WAYS.* of Cosmic Consciousness in form. You do harm to yourself with these self-diminishing attitudes of lack and need, breaking *Ahimsa. Brahmacharya* is also lost because you are not seeing all as divine.

When you move out of alignment with these principles, your troubles go in all directions but when you recognize these pitfalls and step away from them, changing your attitude also assists you in all directions. To have love for yourself as well as others, to feel secure in your own divine nature, to have self-acceptance, contentment and joy in what is aligns you and brings harmony and joy in your life. To have gratitude for all the little joys God has provided in your life, the beauty of a sunrise, the sweet scent of a flower, an opportunity to help another, appreciating all of these brings a bright attitude. Taking time to notice all the kindness given to you in your life, to notice that you are cared for, have food on your table, this gratitude brings you in alignment.

You are provided for in so many ways. When you feel the abundance of unconditional love, what need is there to accumulate so much? However when you feel a lack inside yourself, then to cover that lack you want to acquire and to acquire, to have more and more. Life gets complicated; simplicity vanishes and the practice of *Aparigraha* is lost. When *Aparigraha,* not accumulating beyond your needs, is followed, there is fullness inside. You acknowledge the full-ness of your own life. You acknowledge the fullness of what the Divine has given to you.

When you do this, you do not feel lack, you feel safe in your divine origins and you know that you do not need to have so much money in the bank to be safe. You do not need to have so many possessions to be safe. You do not need to have so much power to be safe, to be loved, to be cared for. You realize all you need is in your natural state of being. Your safety and well-being are in the shower of unconditional love and grace falling on you every moment of every day.

You need not indulge this desire for material accumula-tions. Have what you need to live a comfortable life. Do not engage your fears of not having, for you are always cared for through thick and thin. You know, though the Divine loves you, old age still comes. Illness still comes in people's lives; struggles, trials and difficulties come and eventually death comes to your body. This in no way negates the shower of unconditional grace that is your very Source.

Yet human life is fleeting and the human body frail so that both pain and pleasure exist in this realm; gain and loss are a part of human existence. The pain and sorrow of loss can be very deep indeed. Allow yourself to appreciate the beauty of your own existence, the beauty of the love that is divine, even in the pain of loss and the struggle of sorrow. Good times and bad times come and go in human life but Love Divine is a constant. As you do these practices to train the mind, remember this and look on the bright side of life. Then surely you will lead a happy life and all will be well, even in the hard times of loss and struggle.

Working with the Judgments of Others

Sometimes you may find yourself up against a person or group of people that hold negative opinions or grudges against you. You may be unable to reconcile with the individual or group. As long as you want the acceptance of the person or group, a power is held over you that can harm you. In this situation, go to the God Self, the infinite *Brahma,* and surrender the situation. If there is something you can change, change it. If there is some way you can heal the situation, heal it. If there is nothing you can do, accept it but do not accept the negative words and actions directed at you. Rather accept what is. Let go of your need for approval. Let go of your need for acceptance by others.

Find your approval from the Divine. Find the love of the infinite Being and let that grace shower upon you, filling your heart and mind. Continue to do compassionate actions toward living beings and to serve others as your own true Self. Continue to stay in the bright, eternal light of the Infinite. Surrender your attachments to the Divine.

With that which you can change, be active and dynamic to make positive changes. With that which you cannot change, surrender it to *the Divine.* He is your shelter in the storm. He is your bright light in the dark night. He is the one who will hold your hands as you walk through the Valley of the Shadow of Death. He is the one who will take you home. All those who are diminishing you with their judgments and beliefs are merely children. They are children of the Divine struggling themselves to find their way home, acting out their fears and insecurities, their biases, their prejudices. It is the way of human life, these struggles. If there has been wounding to you and harm to you, surrender it all. Give it all to your cosmic Source and take his shelter. If there is wounding to your heart and mind, following these tenets of *Yama* and *Niyama* will help you to heal the wounds. Surrender your attachment, love yourself unconditionally, let go of resentments, forgive yourself, forgive others, look on the bright side of life, find even the smallest joy or happiness and focus on it. These practices will heal you.

IF THERE IS WOUNDING TO YOUR HEART AND MIND, FOLLOWING THE TENETS OF YAMA AND NIYAMA WILL HELP YOU TO HEAL THE WOUNDS.

Ignorance, *maya*, causes much suffering in this world. Great harm is done to people by other people. Do not be one who does that kind of harm to others. Practice love, compassion and surrender. As you surrender that which has wounded you, slowly, slowly the wounds will heal in your heart. When you look on the bright side and find the joy of your divine family, which is this whole human race, you will begin to see that something small has been taken away so that you might embrace something larger.

Healing Through Kirtan, Surrender and Puja

Many trials and tribulations happen in human life. There are times of happiness and great joy and then there are times of difficulty. During both external and internal struggles, people must face the pressures within, the pains in the heart, the sorrows, the angers and the fears in life. When beset with these difficulties one solution is to do *kirtan,* a practice of singing, chanting and even dancing to the names of God. *Kirtan* always warms the heart. When your mind won't stop racing, chanting the names of God is very beneficial, followed by silent meditation. To dance *kirtan* is even more effective than merely to sing *kirtan* because when you move the body with the music, then a harmony of voice, body and music begins to happen and soon you find you are in a rhythm, a flow. A flow of vital energy moves through the body, as well as through *CHANTING THE NAMES OF GOD IS VERY HEALING FOR DIFFICULT STATES OF MIND.* the voice and the mind, calming troubled thoughts. You are completely engaged, kinesthetically engaged as well as with your voice and mind. When doing these practices, your mind tends to move into a sweet place. Difficult thoughts begin to dissipate.

Chanting the names of God is very healing for difficult states of mind. Rather than ideating upon your difficulty, chant the names of God in *kirtan* and think of the divine presence all around you. This opens your heart in love. It will benefit you greatly, because many difficult moods, whether sorrowful, anxious, angry, regretful, grieving or stimulated by some type of external circumstance are related to thoughts in the mind. The mind goes over these thoughts again and again until it becomes despondent or upset. *Kirtan* will help calm the upset, restless mind, helping direct it away from the stressor and toward the Divine.

There are times, when faced with difficulties in the outer world, you need to sit and evaluate your situation in order to come to a decision. However there are other times when issues in your life only serve to trigger a mood. Then the mood promotes negative thoughts and the thoughts promote negative emotions. The mind goes around and around like a little hamster on a wheel in a cage. It just keeps going, going, going but goes nowhere. You just think, think, think but there is no progress. Why?

Rather than finding a solution by thinking about the issue over and over, you get stuck. Like the hamster on the wheel, the mind gets a lot of mental exercise but there is no progress. It is just an unproductive repetition of thoughts. When that is the case, rather than running on the wheel, it is better to stop and say, "All right, enough." Then play *kirtan*; sing *kirtan*; dance *kirtan*. It will help you a great deal more than thinking. Sometimes the mind requires time to settle down. You might need to chant for twenty or thirty minutes. Chanting the names of God, feel that there is only the one Beloved, the one divine Self, permeating everything. When these feelings are awakened and occupy the mind, where are the problems?

When the mood changes and you feel the presence of the Divine, somehow the problems fly away. Then where are the difficult thoughts? They have flown the mind, and with the thoughts so has the mood. When a problem has solutions, you can take time apart from your meditation to analyze it, find a solution and take action, but when there is no action to be taken and the mind is just going on about it, then it is better to redirect your thoughts in a positive direction.

You can also do this while you are working and engaged

in life. When the mind begins to ruminate on problems, if you chant the names of God internally or silently repeat *mantra* while engaged in activities, then the mind ceases to chatter at itself. It is too busy chanting or saying the mantra. This can be a very beneficial practice. It allows you to take control of your mental activities and direct them toward the Divine, rather than letting your thoughts and emotions overcome you and drag you into difficult mental states.

Yoga is not about suppressing emotions. It is to re-direct the mind and emotions toward the sublime. If inside there is a need to uncover suppressed or buried emotions or reactions, it is important to listen to your own being. When repressed experiences and emotions rise to the surface of the mind, they may overcome you *THERE ARE TIMES WHEN A GOOD CRY IS VERY HEALTHY.* at first, bringing up painful feelings and tears, but these tears lead to a release of emotions and an opening of the heart. Spiritual practices such as *kirtan,* chanting and repeating of *mantras* are not done to suppress mental and emotional reactions and may even bring them to the surface when needed so that you can look at them and let them go.

Recognize the difference between states of mind where you have opportunity to change a situation and states of mind where you have no opportunity for change. Know the difference between habits of mind that allow thoughts to run around in a repetitive circle going nowhere and states of mind where emotions and feelings want to be released, not repeated over and over like a broken record, but need release. There are times when a good cry is very healthy.

There are times to feel your emotions and there are times to take charge and to say, "Enough. Enough of this! Now I offer it to the Divine."

When you feel strong sentiments arising in the mind a very, very good practice is to do *Guru Puja*, a practice of offering everything to God.

Akhanda mandala karam,
Vyaptam yena cara caram
Tatpadam darshitam yena,
Tasmae Shrii Gurave namah.

Ajinana timir andhasya
Jinananin jana shala kaya
Caksurun militam yena
Tasmae shrii Guruve namah

Gurur Brahma, gurur Vishnu
Guru devo Maheshvarah
Gurureva Parama Brahmah
Tasmae Shrii Guruve namah
FROM THE GURU GITA

The meaning of the first stanza is that the entire circle of creation, both moving and unmoving is permeated by the Divine. That one is your nearest and dearest. You surrender all of your difficulties to that One. You pay your deepest respects to the Divine. In the second stanza, we are reminded that it is the One Divine Guru who removes the darkness from the eyes and brings knowledge, understanding and wisdom. To that guru, we pay our salutations and offer our deepest respects, "*Tasmae Shrii Gurave namah*a,"

The third stanza recognizes that the One who permeates the moving and the unmoving, who permeates the entire universe, who gives you knowledge and wisdom, is none other than *Brahma*, the creator, *Vishnu*, the preserver of all existence, and *Maheshvara*, the destroyer of ignorance and illusion. It is none other than *Parama Brahma*, the God of Gods. To that divine Guru, you pay your deepest salutations, "*Tasmae Shrii Guruve namaha.*"

In *Guru Puja* you pay your salutations to that One, you offer everything saying,

Tava dravyam jagat Guru,
Tubhyameva samarpaye

This final stanza of *Guru Puja* acknowledges that all that you have is given by God, the supreme Guru and offers it back to that source from which it has come. "What do I have that you have not given, that is not yours already? What you have given to me, Oh Lord, I give it back to you."

Anything you have held on to, you give back to God in puja. Doing puja every day can be an important part of *sadhana*, spiritual practice, because it brings you to a state of surrender. You begin to let go. All that happens in life is offered in sweet surrender to your Lord, bringing you to a state of peace with yourself. Rather than thinking, "Why does this

WHEN YOU REALLY GIVE ALL YOU ARE HOLDING ONTO WITH YOUR LITTLE EGO, SOMETHING CHANGES.

happen to me?" or, "What's wrong with me?" or, "What's wrong with them?" you think, "It all belongs to you. I return it all. I surrender everything. These things weighing on me do not belong to me, Lord. They belong to You."

In this way, *puja* can assist you to let go and give all to God. When you do this, when you really let go, when you give all you are holding onto with your little ego, something changes. Your struggle in trying to fix all of life's problems finds resolve.

Give all to the divine Lord who permeates this entire universe. Let him or her hold you in Divine arms and remove the veil of ignorance. Let the burdens that belong to her, have come from her, be hers, not yours. Live by Divine will and grace. Then the life becomes sweet. The bitter becomes sweet. The ordinary and mundane becomes sublime. Then love begins to surround you, permeate you, and you realize that this creation is both light and shadow. It is both joy and pain but amidst the joy and pain, the Beloved abides. Both in the light and in the shadows, omnipresent love abides.

You realize you are never alone. You are never helpless. There is in this universe a guiding force for all existence. What guides the stars in the heavens on their path? How can the multitude of living beings arise, exist and fade from existence? There is pattern and form to the universe. There is a grace to all existence. All comes from infinite love, this one eternal Source and all returns to this source.

Are you any different from all the other living beings who struggle to survive, who feel pain and sorrow, who feel joy and happiness, who know the wonders of life and love and the pain of sorrow and loss? Are you any different? Even in your pain, your fear, your struggles, are you not united with all living beings? Offer the play of creation in which you are dancing to the one Beloved. All is from that One, abides within that One and surely will return to that One.

Surrender

That which you think of as yours, your sorrows, your pain, your unique problems, your faults, your shortcomings, are they really yours? In truth, do they not belong to the Divine? This worldly life is said to be a play. The dance of creation, the *Rasa*, like the play of sunlight and shadow through the leaves of a tree, it is an ever-changing tapestry. So, do not take the struggles of your life personally; surrender them all to the Infinite. Give back to that One what is his. Lay these heavy burdens of guilt, shame, self-reproach, inadequacy, sorrow, fear and anger at the feet of the Divine.

Scriptures talk of surrender. They suggest that if you surrender everything to the Divine, to *Parama Purusha*, God, then you attain enlightenment. Self-realization is absolute, complete surrender. When people come to the yogic path they may intend to surrender their ego, even to surrender everything they have, but surrender is very personal. It is being willing to give back to the infinite One your most personal fears, self-reproaches, pains and sorrows. Are they not the hardest to give up? In all honesty are you not attached to the small voice within that criticizes you, that thinks deep down inside, "I am not as good as others. I don't do things right. I have this or that problem"? These beliefs are the real attachment.

People feel they are attached to wealth, name and fame but why do they need wealth, name and fame? Is it not to cover the pain within, to run from the suffering and feelings of smallness inside? Let go. Give these feelings to the Divine. Give your sense of individuality, your sense of I-am, your fundamental feelings of separation to the God within. Surrender these to the Infinite in the practices of *puja*, by doing *kirtan*, singing, chanting the names of God, dancing and then finally by doing deep meditation, letting go of everything until all the illusions fade away and the one Self alone abides.

You ARE BRIGHT BEYOND COMPARISON AND LOVED MORE THAN WORDS CAN POSSIBLY SAY.

You are his child, his nearest and dearest; you are bright beyond comparison and loved more than words can possibly say. Fear not. Let your hearts be bright. Enfold yourself in divine grace and love of the Infinite. Burn your difficulties in the fire of Love Divine. When you find your way to the flame eternal within your heart of hearts; all *samskaras* are burnt, all reactions of mind dissolve.

CHAPTER VII

Integrating the Teachings

The Practice of Dharma and the Web of Life

*D*harma is the way toward essence, the *Tao*. These two concepts from different cultures express a very similar understanding. The *Tao* is the *dharma*, the true law, the true way in which all things move toward their essence and their right place in the matrix of life. Human *dharma* involves seeking our essential nature, our divine origin. It is your natural calling to want to return to wholeness, to your natural

BEGIN TO TRAIN THE MIND TO MOVE WITH DHARMA TOWARD THE DIVINE.

state of being, *sahaja*, to harmony and balance in all things, to where you feel attuned and complete.

The tenets of *Yama and Niyama* were given in ancient times so that a person might begin to train the mind to move with *dharma* toward the Divine. On the individual level, *dharma* requires personal effort and refers to your individual calling in life. However we all share human *dharma* as well, an inner draw toward the Divine.

On the collective level of society, *dharma* requires the efforts of everyone involved to create a social structure that not only supports people's physical well-being, but uplifts their spirits as well. It requires everyone holding the intention to support the development of each person's human potential and the welfare of all beings. Many people believe in the environment, the welfare of animals and the relationship of all life. The influence of *dharma* can be felt when you support the interwoven, interconnected network of life and nurture the interdependent ecosystems that form our world.

From an ecological point of view, it can be seen that there is a web of life that we are all a part of. No one is an island. Everyone is a part of this interdependent network. There is a need for realization of one's place, one's *dharma* in the web of life, for harmony to develop between you and the network of life.

When people loose their connection to *dharma* and are out of balance within themselves, they become out of place in the network of life. Then they create disturbances in the ecosystems and the world goes out of balance. By centering ourselves and harmonizing with the web of life, we have an integrated wholeness that extends even beyond the planet to the stars and the whole cosmos. We all exist in this harmonious web of life. We are all together in this magnificent living connection. All life on the planet is as one organism. The different species function together in an interwoven, interconnected flow.

When following *dharma* you begin to feel wholeness of being. You become connected to the web of life. Then you have something to give to humanity, a capacity that goes beyond ordinary capacities. For it is not your capacity, it is the capacity of the Divine. Be the hands and feet of the Divine in this world and keep your mind ever immersed in unconditional love, in the truth of your being. Then your human potential will be realized and your life will be a great and truly human life.

If you follow *Satya,* and are deeply honest with yourself, having a compassionate heart and the quality of discrimination allows you to distinguish that which leads toward the Great as opposed to that which leads away. This is the best guide for your future actions. This is what allows you to distinguish that which is flowing to the cosmic nucleus from that which fights the stream and moves in the other direction. This sense of discrimination allows you to walk the path of *dharma*. When walking the path of *dharma* you enter into the stream of the divine flow of life toward the cosmic nucleus.

There is no *Dharma* without the Divine. Act with knowledge developed through your practice of *Svadhyaya;* know that all of the capacities you have belong to *Brahma*. For you are a part of *Brahma,* and in this vast complexity of life the movement of *Brahma* is creating all the colors and forms of this manifest universe. The consciousness of *Brahma* is manifesting and experiencing self-awareness in your very own form. *Dharma* is followed when you move toward the Divine and the spiritual path is the path of *dharma*. May your path ever run true and your deep source ever shine bright.

The Practice of Service

Karma yoga (right action) and *seva* (selfless service) are a part of the practice of *Tapas* and the cure for the seeds of selfishness that keep the mind and spirit bound in the interests of the little self. This binding of self-absorption creates a wall between you and your soul and a feeling of smallness that leads to unhappiness. It is truly bondage.

When you dissolve this bondage through practicing *karma yoga,* the feeling of identification with the experience of *I and mine* gets lessened. With regular practice you begin to feel that the welfare of all living beings is your own welfare and your welfare is no different from theirs. To do *karma yoga* is to do *Seva* or service. *Dharma* and *Seva* cannot be separated. One cannot do *seva* without *dharma*. One cannot have *dharma* without *seva,* or real *seva* without *tapas.*

YOU BEGIN TO FEEL THAT THE WELFARE OF ALL LIVING BEINGS IS YOUR OWN WELFARE.

Seva not only entails doing good deeds for others, but doing them with a sense of selflessness, a feeling of good intent toward others and a feeling of service with no desire for something in return. By doing this type of service day in and day out, a person becomes free from the narrowness of the ego, and they begin to feel their connectedness with all beings. The heart becomes wide and expanded. The wounds of selfishness are cleansed from the mind. This brings a sweet and kind approach. One begins to learn the meaning of compassion through doing *seva* or service to others.

Loving kindness, compassion in all acts of service, and motivation for the welfare of others are essential to *seva*. Seva is not limited to any particular action. Even anger can serve others if your intent is correct. Whether any given act is a service depends on your intention. When your intentions are driven by love and compassion you cannot help but do service. Your heart will be too big to remain content without giving something to others. You will not be able to stop yourself from doing *seva* in the physical, mental or spiritual sphere, or even in all three.

Depending on your disposition, there are some types of service that may be better suited for you than others. What type of service is better for you depends on your personal path. Each individual is a unique flower, opening to the vistas of the sublime. Each has a different, unique way to move. If each person moves toward the cosmic nucleus from their own unique vantage point, some will move one way and some another. It may appear as if they move in different directions but they all move toward the same center.

No matter what your personal inclinations are, doing *Seva* is essential. Spread your palms wide and give to all, and then surely you will attain your treasured goal finding divine unity in this very lifetime. You will find that what you have given has not left you empty-handed but has come back to you one hundred fold. If you want the grace of the Divine in your life, serve others, love others and surely that grace will grow stronger and will bloom within you like a lotus flower. Be happy and enjoy the shower of love that your divine Source is ever giving unto you.

The Practice of Love

The most direct experience that the average person has of divinity is the experience of love. In moments of feeling deep love toward another, you may experience a sense of proximity to the Divine. For many people, this is their closest experience, but the quality of the experience depends of the type of love you have.

There are three types of love that most people engage in. The first type of love is just a business deal; "I will love you if you love me or give me what I want." This type of love is conditioned by self-interest because you want something in return. It does not awaken the deeper strata of your being.

The second type of love is still conditioned but more expansive. In this love you love because it gives you pleasure to do so, because it feel good, even wonderful, to love another or to love God. Your love is not dependent on getting something in return but still is conditioned by how much it benefits you. It still feeds the ego identity.

The third type of love that you can develop is love that asks nothing in return but wants only the happiness and welfare of the one that you love. This love is selfless, expansive, unconditioned by self-interest. When this love develops, you love with an entirely open heart that gives freely without thought of what will be given in return. Not even your own enjoyment or happiness is of concern. This love is open and freely given and goes beyond the confines and definitions of the ego. When you experience this love, you begin to transcend your own smallness and touch the Infinite.

Love of the Divine is a love that expects nothing and gives

unconditionally. With anything less, the experience of divinity will escape you for you will not be able to fathom the nature of that One. This is because the Divine is unconditional love. This is the love that *Parama Purusha,* the divine One, has for each and every living being. Whether you are a good person or a bad person, whether you are high-born or low-born, that divine Being loves you unconditionally. Divine love becomes clouded to our perception when we are distracted by self-interest. But

It is best to be as simple as the child, to let love into you, let it permeate you, fill you and use you.

when we love open heartedly, unconditionally, the shower of grace and love that is always there becomes visible.

Love Divine may be known in the experience of awe that might arise in a natural setting; perhaps a feeling of unity and love with all beings might arise and a sense of awe at the great beauty of life. It is in these moments that you begin to connect with the qualities and characteristics of the divine Being. In order to make this pure connection in love, it is best to be as simple as the child, to let love into you, let it permeate you, fill you and use you.

The secret to success is to love others as your own self. Practice harmlessness with deep and undying love of the highest order. Keep your body and mind pure and clean; wash the dust from your body and the dirt from your mind. Make yourself pure of heart. Do kind acts; do not covet what belongs to another and enjoy every act, every thought as the wellspring of divine love. Attribute all to that One. Keep nothing for yourself. Own what you need, but know to whom it belongs and remember your divine Beloved in every action throughout your life. Give yourself to the infinite *Brahma*. This is yoga's secret way to happiness and well-being.

These practices allow us to become positively directed and to open our hearts and minds to more subtle perceptual fields. Fields in which the divine play of love and light reveal our oneness and guides us home to our Source.

The Practice of Happiness

Every living being wants happiness. In each and every human heart is a longing, an innate restless desire to find happiness. Yet when the baby is born, its first response is to cry and to struggle for air. The young one first struggles to breathe, then struggles to learn to use the physical body, to get it to work. There is a struggle from the very beginning of life and this struggle to survive, to thrive, to go forward continues throughout life in one form to another.

A time comes eventually when a person begins to reflect, to look into his or her own heart and experience a yearning for lasting happiness. Every human being wants to avoid suffering. The restlessness in the human heart causes a yearning, a search for happiness that is foundational in human experience. Out of it many desires grow in the mind.

According to one's personal experience, disposition and *karmic* reactions, the desires for happiness appear as different images in the mind. Each and every living being loves its life. Each one wants to exist in this world, wants to continue living and wants to find happiness. No one wants to be without happiness. All living beings are searching for happiness, each in their own way. Each wants to find his or her own path, her own way to joy, to infinite happiness. However, the thoughts that come in the minds of living beings as to what will bring happiness vary a great deal.

For the cat in the wild, it may be a good kill. For a deer, it might be a beautiful field of fresh grasses. For a mother, it might be to hold her baby in her arms. For some people happiness takes the image of material wealth. They feel that if only they had more money, more possessions, a better car, a better house, a better job, then they would finally be happy.

Yet you see, so often many of these ideas about happiness come with the caveat of needing to acquire something that is not there. Once you acquire it, then you think you will be happy. The problem is, once it is acquired, happiness usually only stays for a little while and then again the restlessness comes. Then again you feel you want something more; you need something else to make you happy.

Material success, success in the world and even success in your love relationships, tends to bring happiness but only for a limited time. Generally speaking, the happiness is not long-term. Many times that which has brought you happiness at one time in your life will be the source of suffering at another time of your life when you lose that to which you are attached. Even the physical body ages; the beauty of your face, your hair, the youthfulness of your body can change very rapidly. All that you are attached to in this world will shift and change with the passage of time.

As the restlessness continues, various images get

substituted over time as to what happiness looks like. As mind grows in magnitude, a desire to find a happiness that is lasting begins to emerge. One begins to realize that all the material objects and sensory pleasures will not bring lasting happiness. Even if you build an empire and have utmost success and riches, still happiness can elude you. It does elude people, even rich people. As you reflect, you begin to realize that all of these efforts bring only the temporary pleasure of accomplishment but no lasting happiness.

Then real self-reflection begins. You may wonder why you are here in this life. At that stage the realization often comes that just fulfilling your personal desires is not enough. A yearning begins to emerge to be connected to a larger sense of Self, a cosmic sense of Self. You do not want to feel isolation. You want to experience love. You may begin to want to give something to the world, to make life better for others. A longing for expansiveness arises.

As these subtler yearnings come, the direction of life changes because now building monuments to your power, acquiring financial wealth and success become less significant than acquiring true happiness. Serving others, sharing with others, giving to the world become more important. When you begin to experience giving of yourself in service to others, a sense of something greater, something larger than yourself begins to emerge. You become self-actualizing. You begin to feel an expansion of mind, a great longing within you for union, for wholeness, for the completion of love.

The *yogis* of ancient times, realizing the condition of human existence, took to deep and silent meditation to explore these longings. Those intelligent people sat for meditation to silence the mind, silence the restless desires that want to reach out further and further, again and again, to acquire whatever image symbolizing happiness is in the mind. They looked deep within into the stillness of being. They learned to silence the desires of the mind and make it peaceful, calm and quiet. They learned to make the mind as clear and still as a lake without ripples, the waters not stirred or muddied, to see not only the surface but look into the depths.

When the mind is quieted, stilled in meditation and the restlessness of desire calmed, when you take a moment out of your day to be at peace, your mind like the still, pristine mountain lake, becomes undisturbed, transparent. Being transparent, you can see through the mind to the deeper nature of your own being, to the love that is your essence, which is your natural state of being.

This natural divine state that is your essential being becomes visible to you. That which is within rises to be known, not to be thought about, but to be known. With your feeling, your existence, you know your deeper Self within. Knowing the deeper Self within, you begin to be acquainted with that which is in the innermost recesses of your being. Becoming acquainted with that from which you have come, you lose the disturbance of disconnection and restlessness.

You realize the restlessness is a desire to return to your own Source, to your own natural state of being. That natural state of being is truth, is love Divine. When you see deeply, past the quieted mind to the inner recesses of your being, you become immersed in those inner recesses and you begin to realize that there is an expansiveness of love, an expansiveness of consciousness, an expansive truth, a deeper truth, a more real truth, and it is vast. It is undefined. It is total.

This truth exists beyond all limitations, all definitions. There is an attraction to the Great within each of us. When this attraction, this love dominates your mind and being, then you are ready to dissolve all dualities, all separations and allow yourself to melt into the wholeness of being, into the Source from which you have come.

You are not bound by the outlines of your body, the thoughts that have possessed your mind, your education or by any of the identities that you have acquired. Those are superficial, transitory engagements of your aware-ness. When you sink into this deeper stratum, you will experience the totality of Self,

THE RESTLESSNESS IS THE YEARNING OF YOUR OWN HEART, YOUR OWN SPIRIT, LONGING TO FIND THE WAY HOME.

which is not limited by form and is not defined by your mind or your body. As your awareness becomes immersed in this larger definition of Self, you realize that endless are the forms of the eternal Self. The Self is deathless, ever having been the same through all eternity. The Self is changeless. All the change happens upon the surface of being.

This deep access to your inner being comes when the restless longing within you turns toward love that is eternal, love that lasts. The longing for happiness becomes more focused, more distinct in the subtle realms of the mind. No longer do external objects attract your desire but a longing emerges for inner awakening, inner realization. The longing for the Great emerges. The yearning arises in the mind for oneness with love, with God and the closer you get to that eternal Being, the stronger this desire grows.

It grows until it becomes all-consuming, like a drowning man gasping for air; the yearning for the Infinite in one who comes in close proximity to divinity becomes a madness. It is so powerful that it consumes all other desires. This passion of the heart burns all else in the flames of love. Its intensity of passion can bring the mind into the realm of the Infinite.

But this cannot be done by your efforts alone. It is done by the grace of the divine God Self, that cosmic nucleus of the universe. That cosmic Source is drawing all the living beings unto itself. For those who come in close proximity, it is like coming close to the sun. The fire of it burns everything away and there is dissolution into the eternal One.

If the person continues refining this yearning for true happiness, looking within, he or she becomes single-pointed. Then the person encounters the grace of the Infinite that burns away all other passions from the mind. The small I burned in the passion of love becomes the eternal One, dissolved into the whole. The yearning that is essential in the human heart is fulfilled permanently and eternally. There is a completion, a return to Source, a return home.

Then your search for happiness is no more. The restlessness is gone. For the restlessness is the yearning of your own heart, your own spirit, longing to find your way home, longing to return to the love, to the Source where you are whole, complete, fulfilled. When that is found, this restlessness that has driven you goes away and there is stillness, peace and love is fulfilled.

This journey is the greatest adventure of human life. If you want an adventure, this is the true adventure, the great journey of the human spirit. You can go to Mecca, go on pilgrimage here and there. This is perhaps good exercise for the body and interesting but it is the internal journey to the Mecca of the Infinite that will bring you the greatest success. To do this, follow your yearning for happiness and recognize the illusionary nature of all forms that appear before you. When you sink deep, you will find that the beloved Divinity has taken each of these forms and no form is a separate existence, for all forms are part of the one eternal Self.

Once you begin to realize what it is you truly yearn for, then the door begins to open and grace comes to guide you home. *Yama* and *Niyama* are practices to purify the mind, awaken the heart and help you recognize grace so that you may find your way home to the timeless shores of eternal Being.

CHAPTER VIII

The Work

Practicing the Teachings

Practical suggestions for implementing these teachings have already been given within these writings but many people find it helpful to have very specific exercises to work on. To this end the following suggestions are given.

Practice Awareness and Write it Down

The greatest gift you have in your toolbox for self-development is your ability to focus your attention on something and bring awareness to it. The problem is that many times we tend to operate on autopilot and become unconscious about our daily habits of thought and action.

The practices of *Yama* and *Niyama* challenge us to look at our habitual patterns of thought and behavior and work with them. It takes a lot of intentional awareness to pay attention to these unconscious habits. And our memories are often not so good when it comes to exactly what we have done, because we are not paying attention.

LIVING LOVE

To change this we need a way to bring attention to our habits and then to begin consciously cultivating new ones that we want to have. The best tool that I know of to do this is to write it all down, every day or even at different times during the day.

- *Keep a Yama and Niyama Journal:* It is often handy to keep a journal that is dedicated to your practice of *Yama* and *Niyama*. Start each day by observing your thoughts and behavior in relation to each of the areas of focus of *Yama* and *Niyama*.

- *Practice Self-Assessment:* Every morning set an intention to notice your adherence to the practices throughout your day and then in the evening or when you have time, write down what you have observed. Ask yourself the following questions or similar questions tailored to your life and then write down your answers. Remember that you may include people and the other living beings that surround us as well, the animals and plants.

  o *Ahimsa:* Have my thoughts or actions injured anyone today? Have I been sensitive to the thoughts and feelings of others? Have there been ways in which I have shown kindness to another today?

  o *Satya:* Have I been truthful with others today? Did I exaggerate or tell a little white lie? If so what did it get me? Have I used my words with kindness so as not to hurt anyone? How could I have been more truthful and still have been kind with my words today?

  o *Asteya:* Have I taken anything today that belongs to another? Have I secretly wanted to be like someone else or have what they have? Have I been jealous? How could I have given more generously today?

- *Brahmacharya:* Have I seen the Divine in all that I desire today? Have I noticed the divine nature of all beings? Have I practiced *Madhuvidya*, sweet knowledge? How could I have changed my outlook?
- *Aparigraha:* Have I been greedy today or stingy? Or have I been generous? Have I accumulated things I don't need? How could I have lived with more simplicity today?
- *Saucha:* Have I practiced cleanliness today in my personal self-care and in my relationship to my environment? Have I exercised and eaten healthy food? How about fasting? Have I kept my thoughts and actions pure and sentient? How could I have improved my practice?
- *Santosha:* Have I maintained equanimity today? What have I done to maintain mental peace and contentment today? How successful have I been? What thoughts or situations have disturbed my peace? How could I have responded differently?
- *Tapas:* Have I noticed the needs of others today? Did I go out of my way to help someone? What were my motives? Did I want something in return? How might I have done more for others today?
- *Svadhyaya:* Did I take time-out today to read something inspiring or listen to a spiritual talk? Have I engaged in deep self-reflection and study today? How might I improve in this practice?
- *Ishvara Pranidhana:* Have I taken the time to remember the Divine today? Have I done my meditation? Have I taken the time to feel divine grace in my life? What might I have done to improve my practice?

- *Work on Your Practice:* Once you have got your observation process down and are able to bring your attention to the practices, you are ready to begin focusing on self-improvement. For this stage it may be better to take one practice at a time and develop it while continuing your journal observation process of *Yama* and *Niyama*.
  - o *Observe:* Observe your practice in the area you want to work on.
  - o *Analyze:* Analyze your strengths in the practice and notice where your areas of weakness are. Figure out what you can do in your life circumstances to enhance your practice.
  - o *Act:* Put it to the test. Put your ideas into action during your daily interactions and see what happens.
  - o *Integrate:* Then write about your experience and refine it. See how you might do it better or more. Or how you might adjust your practice to be more realistic. Don't give up. If at first you don't succeed in living up to what you want to do, pick yourself up and begin again. Every day is a new dawn, a new beginning. Keep at it and believe in yourself.
  - o *Keep Going:* When you are ready, perhaps after one or two weeks, move on to focus on another area of the *Yama* or *Niyama* practice. Continue on like this until you have gone through all the *Yama* and *Niyama* practices.
  - o *Reflect:* Then take a look back at where you started, read over your earlier journal entries and see what has changed. Give yourself some credit. Appreciate your good work.
  - o *Continue the Practice:* At this point the areas you still

need to pay special attention to will become very clear to you. Remember this is a life-long practice. Like focusing a lens, it gets clearer and clearer with continued adjustment.

Suggestions for Incorporating Yama and Niyama

- *Cultivate the Opposite:* In the *Yoga Sutras* of Patanjali, it suggests that if you have a tendency you want to change, that you intentionally cultivate responding with the opposite approach. For example if you tend to be a bit stingy or greedy, consciously begin to respond to people with generosity in the situations that would normally evoke greed. Or if you tend to evade and avoid by telling people what you think will satisfy them instead of the truth, which might make you accountable, instead be completely transparent and honest. Changing your responses will not be comfortable at first but will allow you to cultivate new and more healthy patterns of behavior. Give it a try!

- *Look on the Bright Side:* Cultivating a positive psychology in life, noticing what is going well and right with life instead of what is wrong goes a long way toward uplifting your spirit and creating a much happier life. The practices of forgiveness, generosity, and compassion are part of this positive approach. It may be hard when you are feeling down and discouraged but give it a try and you will notice a difference. When it becomes a habit it will change your life.

- *Do Something for Someone Else:* This is *Seva*, service. When you make it part of your daily activities it makes a difference. It doesn't mean you have to go out and feed the poor every day, though that is good to do. There are many ways to do service both big and small. Figure out how you can incorporate it in your life and put it in practice!

- *Affirm Your Intentions:* In your *Yama* and *Niyama* journal, write down in positive terms those intentions or actions you really want to incorporate in your life. For example if you want to increase loving kindness you may affirm. "I am loving and kind to everyone I meet." Work with these affirmations until they feel really right for you and then say them every day. Even write them down and put them where you can see them, like on your bathroom mirror, refrigerator or a similar noticeable place.

- *Have a Practice Chart:* Some people find it helpful to have a practice chart where you can list the activities you want to incorporate and check them off as you do them. It is a good way to stay conscious. For example you may list each day meditation, yoga, eating good meals, keeping my room clean, and so on. Then have the days of the week and check off each day you do your desired practice.

- *Take Care of Yourself:* Seems easy but for many of us self-care can get put on the back burner and forgotten. Then when your body is not in good shape and you're stressed and strained, everything else you are doing suffers. So as part of your *Yama* and *Niyama* practice be sure to include self-care practices. How we are with others begins at home with how we treat ourselves.

- *Meditate and Practice Being Connected:* The big resource

that we all share and that can carry us through the storms of life is our connection to our divine Source. Take time each day to nurture that connection with regular meditation, going beyond your thoughts and ideas into the stillness of being, into the light of the eternal God Self. Set a regular place. A regular time for your practice once, or better yet, twice a day. Make a commitment to doing it, no matter what. Set aside the time each day and just sit until it becomes a habit. Then a time will come when you just don't feel right if you haven't meditated. If you have trouble concentrating maybe read a bit of spiritual inspiration or do yoga postures beforehand. And surrender everything to the one eternal divine Self.

Behavioral Exercises

Below are some examples of the types of activities you might want to begin to cultivate into your practices. These are just a few examples to help you think of what you might want to do to enhance your practice of the profound principles of *Yama* and *Niyama*.

- *Tapas:* Make a commitment to do at least one kind act, no matter how small, for someone else every day. Look for opportunities through your day. Then at the end of the day write down your random acts of kindness. Grow your ability to notice others and to do *Seva*.
- *Satya:* Make an effort to be honest in what you say and do. Live in integrity and be true to your word all day, every day. Notice whether there are times you tend to

evade, avoid, exaggerate or outright lie to get something you want or to get out of something you do not want to do. Then make a conscious effort to be direct and tell the truth. Be true to your word. If you say you will do it, do so, no matter how difficult. If you can't do it or really don't intend to, say so, even if it is embarrassing. Stand in your truth. Don't be mean in how you say it. Don't blame others or get angry or hurtful. Just say honestly where you are with each situation. You will be amazed how it clears the air. It may be uncomfortable at first but soon you will feel the good feeling that comes when living in integrity.

- *Santosha:* Observe how many times a day you feel that little, or sometimes big, tension inside when you lose your equanimity and sense of well-being and slip into unconscious reactions to life circumstances. Then later analyze each situation and see if you had choices, if you could have stayed centered and calm, not gotten ruffled. Then make a practice of noticing when the feeling just begins and changing your response. If you need to take space, view it all with detachment, not getting caught in someone else's efforts to draw you into drama. Do what works to stay balanced. Meditate, surrender it all to the Divine, let go and trust. Infuse your view of life with positivity and joy until you find contentment and well-being. Practice each day and write in your journal. Life can get a whole lot better!

These are just a few ideas for putting these profound and life changing principles into practice. What are your ideas? Go for it!

Om Shanti, Shanti, Shanti

Living Love: Yama & Niyama
Thoughts & Observations

Living Love: Yama & Niyama
Thoughts & Observations

Living Love: Yama & Niyama
Thoughts & Observations

Living Love: Yama & Niyama
Thoughts & Observations

Glossary of Sanskrit Terms

Ahimsa: Not to inflict pain or suffering on another intentionally.

Aparigraha: Not to accumulate beyond one's needs.

Asteya: Not to steal from or deprive another of their due.

Ashtanga Yoga: The eight fold path of yoga including *Yama, Niyama, Asana, Pranayama, Pratyahara, Dharana, Dhyana, and Samadhi.*

Bhakti: Devotion to God.

Bhava: Devotional state of absorption in the Divine

Brahma: Cosmic existence. Composed of both the unmanifest Purusha (Consciousness) and manifest Prakriti (nature). The universe. God.

Brahmacharya: To see everything as the manifestation of the Divine.

Dharma: The way or path toward your eternal Source. The law or order of things.

Brahma Sadhana: Meditation upon the Divine.

Guru: One who leads from darkness to light. An enlightened master. A teacher.

Ishvara Pranidhana: To practice concentrated ideation upon the Divine. Surrender to God

Karma: Expressed reactions to past actions or experiences. Reactions that have been held latent in the subconscious mind (*samskaras*) and are now manifest.

Koshas: Layers of the mind. There are five koshas or layers of mind in *Tantra. Hiranyamaya* or *Anandamaya Kosha,* the bliss body, *Vijnanamaya Kosha* the knowledge body, *Atimanas Kosha* the intuitional realm, *Manomaya Kosha* the mind,

Kamamaya Kosha the desires, and *Anumaya Kosha* the physical body.

Mantra: a word or grouping of words with a sacred meaning that is either said internally or out loud to focus the mind in meditation.

Om: The seed sound of all creation.

Purusha: Cosmic Consciousness.

Parama Purusha: Supreme, highest Consciousness.

Sadvipra: A highly evolved soul that identifies with no group or class but relates to all living beings as part of a whole.

Satya: Truth said with kindness and nonviolence.

Sadhana: Spiritual practice; meditation.

Sadhaka: One who does spiritual practices.

Sahaja: The natural state of being. Consciousness, Self.

Samskara: Reactions to past actions held within the subconscious mind, waiting to be expressed.

Santosha: To maintain equanimity of mind through contentment.

Saucha: To maintain purity of mind through cleanliness.

Satsanga: The company of spiritual people. A spiritual community. Also called *samgha*.

Shanti: Deep spiritual peace.

Svadhyaya: To acquire knowledge of reality.

Tantra: The science of subtle energy that liberates the mind from darkness and expands consciousness. (Not a sexual practice)

Tapas: To practice selflessness in service to others.

Viveka: Discriminating understanding. Knowing the real unified nature of all rather than seeing only separate forms.

Yoga: To yoke or unite the small self to the One, the unitary whole God Self.

About the Author

*I*n addition to being an author, Maetreyii Ma Nolan is a licensed psychologist with a doctorate in Transpersonal Psychology, a teacher of yogic philosophy and ancient wisdom, an ERYT 500 Yoga Teacher, and an ordained yogic minister, or *Acharya*.

She is the co-founder and past president of Ananda Seva Mission and a former director of and teacher in the Ananda Seva Yoga Teacher Trainings and Yoga Therapy certification trainings. Dr. Nolan was also a former director of the Spiritual Emergence Network and a founding member of the Kundalini Research Network.

Maetreyii Ma is currently the president of Ananda Guru Kula, a non-profit organization dedicated to spreading the wisdom teachings of yoga and a psychologist in private practice. She spends her time giving *Baba Talks*, teaching and publishing books of these beautiful discourses and giving retreats and seminars. She currently resides with her family in their ashram community in the northern California San Francisco Bay Area.

Other Publications by Maetreyii Ma

Available Books & Booklets

COMING SOON!
The Rasa Lila: A Feminine Path to God

AVAILABLE NOW
Feminine Mysticism:
Secrets of the Empowered Feminine

The Future is Bright: *Visions of the Future*

The Fundamental Principles of PROUT

Yoga Psychology: *Kundalini and Subtle Body*

FOR ORDERING INFORMATION CONTACT

Ananda Guru Kula Publications
P.O. Box 9655
Santa Rosa, CA 95405
To Write: anandagurukula@gmail.com
To Call: 707-575-0886

For more information go to: **www.yogama.info**

To find out more about new books and upcoming events,
join our mailing list at **www.yogama.info/contact-me**

Follow us on facebook at **facebook.com/FeminineMysticism**

Follow us on Goodreads at **goodreads.com/
search?a=maetreyii+ma**

Made in the USA
Middletown, DE
14 February 2021